# STUDENT UNIT GUIDE

## NEW EDITION

## AQA AS Sociology Unit 2

### Education and Sociological Methods

Emma Jones and Marsha Jones

Series editor: Joan Garrod

**PHILIP ALLAN**

Philip Allan Updates, an imprint of Hodder Education, an Hachette UK company, Market Place, Deddington, Oxfordshire OX15 0SE

*Orders*
Bookpoint Ltd, 130 Milton Park, Abingdon, Oxfordshire OX14 4SB
tel: 01235 827827
fax: 01235 400401
e-mail: education@bookpoint.co.uk
Lines are open 9.00 a.m.–5.00 p.m., Monday to Saturday, with a 24-hour message answering service. You can also order through the Philip Allan Updates website: www.philipallan.co.uk

ISBN 978-1-4441-6275-2

First printed 2012
Impression number 5 4 3 2 1
Year 2016 2015 2014 2013 2012

Cover photo: Morganimation/Fotolia

Typeset by Integra, India

Printed in Dubai

Hachette UK's policy is to use papers that are natural, renewable and recyclable products and made from wood grown in sustainable forests. The logging and manufacturing processes are expected to conform to the environmental regulations of the country of origin.

P2029

# Contents

## Content Guidance

## Questions & Answers

# Getting the most from this book

**Examiner tips**
Advice from the examiner on key points in the text to help you learn and recall unit content, avoid pitfalls, and polishy your exam technique in order to boost your grade.

**Knowledge check**
Rapid-fire questions throughout the Content Guidance section to check your understanding.

**Knowledge check answers**
**1** Turn to the back of the book for the Knowledge check answers.

**Summary**

## Summaries
● Each core topic is rounded off by a bullet-list summary for quick-check reference of what you need to know.

## Questions & Answers

Exam-style questions

Examiner comments on the questions
Tips on what you need to do to gain full marks, indicated by the icon **e**.

Sample student answers
Practise the questions, then look at the student answers that follow each set of questions.

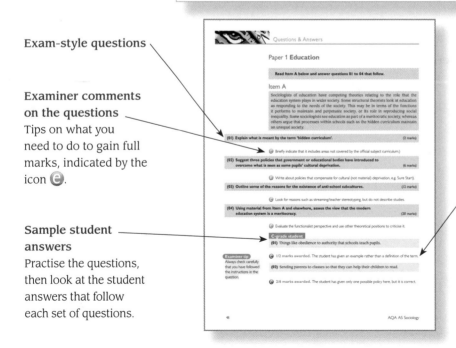

Examiner commentary on sample student answers
Find out how many marks each answer would be awarded in the exam and then read the examiner comments (preceded by the icon **e**) following each student answer.

AQA AS Sociology

# About this book

This guide is for students following the AQA AS Sociology course. It deals with the Module 2 topic **Education and Sociological Methods** and provides an overview of the main areas within the topic.

There are two main sections to this guide:

- **Content Guidance** — this provides details of Unit 2 (SCLY2) Education and Sociological Methods. The exam questions on Education are based on any aspect within the specification, so do not leave out any areas in your revision. Each topic area examines **key ideas**, stating the main points of evaluation and listing the **key concepts** and **key thinkers**. The defined words are key concepts from the specification for this module.
- **Questions and Answers** — this shows you the kind of questions you can expect in the examination. The first three question papers are each followed by two sample answers (a C-grade and an A-grade response). These have examiner comments so that you can see how the marks are allocated. The fourth question paper is for you to attempt yourself.

# How to use the book

Read the Content Guidance section to become familiar with the topic. In order to get full advantage from the Question and Answer section, wait until you have finished studying these topics. When you are ready take each question in turn, and write full answers. When you have done this, compare the A-grade student's answer with your own, paying close attention to the examiner's comments. With the C-grade student, use the examiner's comments as a guide to revise the answers in order to gain higher marks.

Do not be tempted to try to answer all the questions quickly. It is better to focus on one at a time, and spread the work over several weeks. As well as using the questions to consolidate your knowledge and develop your exam skills, you could use some of the questions as revision practice. Reading through the A-grade answers should help your revision.

The AS specification is shown in detail on the AQA website: www.aqa.org.uk. Follow the links to Sociology (2190).

# Content Guidance

This section outlines the major issues and themes of **Education and Sociological Methods**. These are offered as guidance only; there are other concepts and studies that may be relevant.

The content of **Education** falls into five main areas:

- the role and purpose of education, including vocational education and training today
- differential educational achievement of social groups by social class, gender and ethnicity today
- relationships and processes within schools, including: teacher/pupil relationships, pupil subcultures, the hidden curriculum, and the organisation of teaching and learning
- the significance of educational policies, including selection, comprehensivisation and marketisation, for an understanding of the structure, role, impact and experience of education
- the application of sociological research methods to the study of education

You will be tested on:

- quantitative and qualitative methods of research; their strengths and limitations; research design
- sources of data, their strengths and limitations
- differences between primary and secondary, and quantitative and qualitative data
- the relationship between perspectives and sociological methods; the nature of 'social facts'
- theoretical, practical and ethical considerations influencing choice of topic and method(s) and how these methods can be applied to the study of an issue within education

# Explanations of the role and purpose of education, including vocational education, in contemporary society

## Functionalism

### Key ideas

- This is the earliest sociological theory that attempted to explain how social order was possible.
- Education is seen as the main agency of secondary socialisation, taking over as the focal socialising agency after the family. Children are socialised by their families and later by their schools, into the value consensus.
- In school, children are judged by the universalistic standards of society rather than the particularistic values of the home. At school, each student is treated as an individual on their own merits; whereas at home children are related to as sons/daughters/brothers/sisters etc.
- Education is meritocratic. This means that it acts as a neutral filter ensuring that all pupils receive education suited to their natural aptitudes. Those who achieve do so through their own talents, attitudes and application to work.
- Education performs the vital task of role allocation. The most able and talented must be filtered into the most functionally important positions in society.
- Education reinforces social solidarity in society.

**Social solidarity**
Individuals feel that they are part of the whole society.

### Evaluation

- + Identifies education as an integral part of the social structure.
- + Acknowledges the vital role of education as an agency of secondary socialisation.
- + Identifies the needs of modern industrial societies to have an appropriately skilled workforce produced by the education system.
- − Marxists argue that:
  - meritocracy is a myth, transmitted by the ruling class to make the system appear to be fair and just
  - education transmits the values and ideology of the dominant class
  - education reproduces the next generation of workers for capitalism

**Knowledge check I**
Define 'value consensus'.

**Examiner tip**
Functionalist thinking is still relevant today. The coalition government's idea of the 'Big Society' is a functionalist idea.

**Key concepts**

meritocracy; role allocation; secondary socialisation; social solidarity; norms and values

**Key thinkers**

Durkheim, Parsons, Davis and Moore

> **Knowledge check 2**
>
> Define 'meritocracy'.

# Marxism

## Key ideas

- Class conflict is at the root of society.
- Meritocracy is a myth.
- Education is a major agency of social control in modern capitalist society.
- The education system is an **ideological state apparatus** that brainwashes children into docility and obedience.
- The hidden curriculum ensures that the values and ideology of the dominant class are internalised as natural and normal by pupils.
- Education reproduces the next generation of workers for capitalism.
- The relationship between teachers and pupils mirrors the exploitative relationship between bosses and workers.
- The economic infrastructure exerts considerable influence over the schooling system. There is a close correspondence between the needs of capitalism and the schooling system.
- The class system is reproduced through the schooling system. Educational inequality is systematic and the real task of the schooling system is to filter working-class pupils into working-class jobs. Middle-class pupils are filtered into middle-class jobs and the professions.

> **Ideological state apparatus (ISA)** A system like education or religion that legitimates the power of the bourgeoisie (Althusser).

> **Cultural reproduction** A Marxist concept which describes social class relationships as being reproduced from generation to generation.

> **Knowledge check 3**
>
> Identify three aspects of the hidden curriculum.

## Evaluation

- + Identifies the education system as shaped by structural factors. Recognises the influence of the economy in how education is shaped and delivered.
- + Much sociological research supports the Marxist claim that working-class pupils are not encouraged to succeed in school.
- + Recognises the importance of ideology in education.
- + Identifies the myth of meritocracy.
- − The focus is too class-based. Gender and ethnicity tend to be ignored.
- − Overemphasises docility and obedience from pupils. Bowles and Gintis, as well as Althusser, have tended to underestimate pupil resistance to teachers and school.
- − Overstates the close connection between the needs of capitalism and the type of school system.

## Key concepts

cultural capital; cultural reproduction; hidden curriculum; ideological state apparatus; myth of meritocracy; reproduction of workers for capitalism; social control

## Key thinkers

Bowles and Gintis, Bourdieu, Boudon, Althusser, Willis, Braverman

**Knowledge check 4**

What is meant by 'ideology'?

# Feminism

## Key ideas

- Gender inequalities are at the root of society.
- Education reproduces patriarchal power in society.
- The curriculum is still biased in favour of white middle-class male knowledge.
- Textbooks and reading schemes still have a male bias.
- Teachers of both sexes give boys more classroom attention than they give girls.
- The hidden curriculum reinforces gender socialisation.
- Subject choice in secondary school is still gendered.
- Sexual harassment of girls and women teachers by male pupils is a major feature of mixed schools.
- Despite the introduction of the National Curriculum, gender stereotyping in education is still widespread.

**Gendered subject choice** There is a visible bias in the subjects boys and girls choose to study (e.g. languages attract more girls).

## Evaluation

+ Identifies the education system as a major agency of gender socialisation.
+ Identifies gender as a key factor in educational inequality.
+ Feminist studies indicated that boys demanded and received more teacher-time than girls.
+ Identifies the fact that power in society is patriarchal.
− Traditional feminist explanations focused on the reasons for the perceived underachievement of girls, but this is seen as less relevant today as girls have been outperforming boys over the past 20 years.
− Boys are now the underachievers. Recent feminist research has focused on the coping strategies of girls in school, their identity formation and career options.
− Girls' attitudes towards the importance of education have changed (see Sharpe's study).

### Key concepts

gender socialisation; male domination of the classroom; patriarchal curriculum; sexual harassment; subject choice

**Knowledge check 5**

What is meant by patriarchy?

### Key thinkers

Sharpe, Spender, Kelly, Stanworth, Deem, Jones and Mahony, Delamont, Lees

**Knowledge check 6**

Identify three examples of the marketisation of education.

# The New Right

## Key ideas

- This is both a political and a sociological perspective.
- Market forces should be introduced into schooling. Successful schools are rewarded with higher budgets to increase their roll while failing schools are closed down. Schools are encouraged to compete in the marketplace for clients (that is, pupils).
- There is an increased focus on vocational education and preparing pupils for the world of work. The introduction of General National Vocational Qualifications (GNVQs), compulsory work experience for year 10 pupils and the National Record of Achievement (NRA) for all year 11 pupils were implemented in order to achieve this.
- National testing at the various key stages was introduced.
- League tables to show comparative results for schools are published.
- Schools have greater control over their budgets and less involvement with the local education authority (LEA).
- Parents have the right to choose the school to which they would like to send their child.
- A greater focus is put on school inspection to ensure rising standards in all state schools.
- Any secondary school is allowed to apply for academy status and the setting up of 'free schools' by parents and interested parties is encouraged.

**Knowledge check 7**

Identify three New Right educational policies since 2010.

**Examiner tip**

Many commentators have concentrated on the negative aspects of the New Right reforms. However, it is important to produce a balanced argument in order to gain top marks.

## Evaluation

+ The reforms give parents more information about the performance of their children's schools.
+ Ofsted identifies schools with particular problems and suggests and monitors improvements.
+ Schools are more aware of the needs of employers.
− Stephen Ball et al. argue that New Right reforms to education have served to make education less egalitarian and far more divisive, because they give an advantage to middle-class parents.
− Marxists such as Finn argue that the focus on new vocationalism and youth training is simply reproducing young workers for capitalism who have been socialised into the right attitudes and are ready for exploitation.
− British children are subjected to more tests than their European counterparts.

**Key concepts**

academies and free schools; competition; league tables; marketisation of education; parental choice; pupil testing; standards, training, vocationalism

**Key thinkers**

Chubb and Moe, Finn, Ball

# Interactionism

## Key ideas

- Interactionists examine education from a micro-perspective — inside schools. The focus is on the day-to-day running of schools and the interaction between teachers and pupils and between pupils within the classroom.
- The classroom is constructed and constantly renegotiated through interaction between teachers and pupils. Pupils are not passive recipients of teachers' knowledge, but actively participate in learning and resistance.
- Teachers play a crucial role in the success of their students, because they can affect the self-concepts and self-esteem of students.
- The labelling and typing of students by teachers can lead to the creation of self-fulfilling prophecies.
- Streaming and setting have significant effects on the success of pupils in school. There is a close relationship between banding and the social-class background of pupils.
- Some pupils resist the school system. This resistance takes different forms, varying from active rebellion and aggression to subtle adaptations of behaviour.
- Peer groups are seen as having considerable influence on some pupils. This influence can have positive or negative effects on behaviour and achievement.

**Typing** A three-stage process of speculation, elaboration and stabilisation whereby teachers classify and label pupils.

**Knowledge check 8**

(a) What is the difference between streaming and setting?

(b) What is meant by the 'self-fulfilling prophecy'?

### Evaluation

- + Interactionists have challenged the rather deterministic approaches of Marxism and functionalism to education.
- + They have provided valuable insights into the day-to-day running of schools and the reality of the classroom.
- + They have demonstrated the importance of teachers and pupil subcultures in the success or failure of their pupils.
- − Interactionists have been accused of determinism in their approach to education. They presume that once a label has been applied to somebody, a self-fulfilling prophecy will follow.
- − The narrow focus on interaction within the school ignores the importance of wider structural constraints in educational success.
- − Many ethnographic studies tend to be descriptive rather than explanatory.

### Key concepts

interaction; labelling; negotiation; pupil adaptations; pupil subcultures; self-concept; self-fulfilling prophecy; typing; resistance

### Key thinkers

Becker, Hargreaves, Hester and Mellor, Keddie, Rosenthal and Jacobson, Woods, Ball

# Vocationalism

- Vocationalism (work-related learning) is the link between education and the labour market. It stems from the belief that education should be the training ground for employment (often associated with ideas of the New Right).
- Education and training should help to promote economic growth by teaching the skills needed by the workforce.
- In the 1980s, a 'new vocationalism' developed under the Conservative governments led by Margaret Thatcher, during which a number of new measures were introduced.
- The Technical and Vocational Education Initiative (TVEI) (1983) was extended nationally for all 14- to 18-year-old students. It emphasised the importance of work experience.
- The Certificate of Pre-Vocational Education (CPVE) (1985). Less academic students were taught practical skills to prepare them for employment.
- National Vocational Qualifications and General National Vocational Qualifications (**NVQs** and GNVQs) (1993) still remain. They include leisure and tourism, business, information technology, health and social care.
- Youth Training Schemes (YTSs) were designed as employment training for school leavers who were able to gain work-related qualifications.

**NVQs** Qualifications introduced to enhance the training skills of young people and improve vocational education.

### Evaluation

- + Some commentators argue that education standards need to be as high as possible in order to produce a 'magnet economy', where the skills and productivity of the workforce will encourage overseas investment.
- + Instituting appropriate skills training and retraining programmes will give individuals better chances of finding employment.
- + It could be a means of increased opportunities as skill inequalities will be reduced.
- – They are used to restrict the number of workers joining trade unions, in this way reducing the potential bargaining power of the unions.
- – The trainees are a source of cheap labour.
- – The trainees are not counted as unemployed even though they have no guarantee of paid employment after the scheme is over.
- – New workers are kept in 'suspended animation' until jobs become available.

- Trainees are substitutes for full-time workers who would have to be paid more.
- Trainees are potentially de-skilled by being taught 'behavioural etiquette' rather than transferable skills — in this way they have been prepared for disempowerment.
- Many higher education institutions regard vocational qualifications as inferior to academic qualifications.

## Key concepts

youth training schemes; TVEI; NVQs; GNVQs

## Key thinkers

Finn, Bates et al., Yeomans

After studying this section you should be able to explain the role and purpose of education, including vocational education and training, in contemporary society. You should be familiar with the major perspectives:

● Functionalism focuses on the positive contributions education makes to the maintenance and perpetuation of society.

● Marxism focuses on the ways in which the education system reproduces the social relations of production (the class system), legitimating the power of elite groups.

● Feminism focuses on gender relations, seeing the education system as part of a patriarchal society.

● Interactionism focuses on relationships and processes within schools.

Summary

# Sociological explanations of the differential educational achievements of social groups by social class, gender and ethnicity

## Social class

### Outside-school explanations

#### Poverty and material deprivation leading to poor educational achievement

Poverty and low income are likely to result in fewer books, educational toys and lack of computer access in the home. There may be overcrowding and limited space to study at home. Poverty might result in damp homes that can lead to illness and time off school. Jesson and Gray's 1991 Nottinghamshire study identified a clear correlation between poverty and material deprivation. Half of the pupils receiving free school meals attained GCSE scores below 15 points as opposed to one sixth of pupils who paid for meals. Phillips (2001) argued that 'socially excluded' pupils are not simply poor, but the consequence of anti-education family attitudes and values and a state system that both encourages dependency and undermines individual responsibility (underclass theory). Various governments have used different strategies or compensatory education, for example, educational priority areas (EPAs), to try to reverse the effects of deprivation.

### Home factors and parental interest

Douglas saw parental interest as the single most important factor affecting pupil progress. He argued that in general, middle-class parents were more interested in the progress of their children than were working-class parents. Parental interest was measured by visits to the school and how teachers viewed parents. However, he failed to take into account different work practices of parents and differential knowledge of the education system. Unlike many working-class parents, many middle-class parents, especially mothers, invest 'emotional labour' in their children's education.

### Culture clash

Cultural deficit theorists argue that working-class families place greater emphasis on immediate gratification and the need to find employment at the minimum school leaving age, whereas middle-class families place greater emphasis on educational success and staying on post-16. Some working-class pupils may face a 'culture clash' between the values of home and school.

## Language difference

Bernstein identified two different speech codes: the elaborated and **restricted codes**. He argued that working-class pupils are generally socialised into a restricted language code where meanings are context-bound and sentences short with limited vocabulary. Middle-class children, however, have access to both codes. As the language of the school and teachers is of an elaborated nature, this benefits middle-class pupils.

**Elaborated code** A form of speech characterised by complexity. It is context-free so can refer to abstract ideas. It is the language of education and advantages middle-class children.

## Cultural capital

According to Bourdieu, inequalities in power and wealth in society account for inequalities in educational achievement. Children from middle- and upper-class backgrounds are socialised into the dominant culture and possess cultural capital. The dominant class has the power to impose its culture and values as legitimate and the curriculum reflects these values and interests.

Working-class children are filtered out of the education system at the earliest school leaving age through failure in examinations, and self-elimination. Recent research by Reay et al. (2008 ongoing) has shown the continuing significance of cultural capital to achievement. Middle-class students in underachieving schools still do very well, and in many cases do better than similar students in predominantly middle-class schools, because the schools treat them as potential achievers.

**Examiner tip**
Students often confuse the concepts of material and cultural capital. It is extremely important that you are secure with the differences between the two.

## Positional theory

Marxist Raymond Boudon argues that educational inequality is inevitable because of social stratification. Students start school from very different positions, depending on their class. Boudon refers to a cost–benefit analysis of education, whereby studying for higher education may have very different consequences for a middle-class student than for a working-class student. From 2012, university tuition fees are set to rise to a maximum of £9,000 per annum. A working-class student who goes to university, particularly Oxford or Cambridge, will also encounter a significantly different culture from that of home. Working-class students might therefore resist or reject higher education.

# Inside-school explanations

## Labelling and self-fulfilling prophecy

Teachers are middle class by profession and will generally support middle-class values and attitudes. These values may well be at odds with those of some working-class children.

Becker's work demonstrated that teachers tended to see middle-class pupils as those closer to the ideal. Keddie's work showed that social class and streaming are closely linked. Teachers withheld knowledge essential for success from working-class students believing that they could not handle such complex knowledge.

Teachers might stereotype working-class pupils as unlikely to stay on and therefore have lower expectations of these pupils. This may well lead to a self-fulfilling prophecy whereby those children will become less interested in what schooling has to offer and give up on education.

The introduction of league tables has inadvertently discouraged the progress of lower-ability students. Robinson (1998) demonstrated that although overall rates of achievement had risen, the lower-ability pupils had suffered because teachers concentrate on moving potentially grade-D GCSE students to grade-Cs and neglect those who are lower down the achievement ladder. This is educational triage.

### Key concepts

economic capital; cultural capital; elaborated and restricted language codes; **immediate** and **deferred gratification**; fatalism; cultural reproduction; meritocracy; educational triage

### Key thinkers

Halsey, Bernstein, Douglas, Bourdieu, Ball, Keddie, Sugarman, Hyman, Willis, Becker, Rist, Boudon, Reay

# Gender

## Gender issues before 1980

- Sociological explanations of gender and educational achievement before the 1980s focused on the underachievement of girls.
- The educational ideology reflected that of the wider, patriarchal society which emphasised the domestic role of women. As a result, many girls (apart from a few who went on to be university-educated) were encouraged to take up those subjects that would fit them for their assumed future roles as wives and mothers.
- Selection for the tripartite system by 11-plus examination was not an equitable system, as many grammar school places which should have been taken by girls were given to boys in order to even up the numbers of boy and girl pupils. Girls' results were weighted downwards to give boys an equal chance of a grammar school place.
- The career aspirations of girls were seen as less significant than those of boys.
- Socialisation practices at home were seen as detrimental to the career prospects of girls. Gender socialisation encouraged passivity and gentleness in girls and aggression and an instrumental attitude in boys.
- Research into school socialisation focused on reading schemes (Lobban) and discovered a considerable amount of gender-stereotyped material.

**Immediate gratification** Inability to wait for future rewards and wanting to take them as soon as possible.

**Deferred gratification** The ability to put off rewards in the present for greater rewards in the future.

**Knowledge check 10**

Give three examples of differences in gender socialisation.

# Gender issues after 1980

- Over the past three decades, there has been a significant increase in the achievement of girls, especially at GCSE. New explanations have been put forward as to why this reversal of fortunes has taken place and the focus has changed to explaining the underachievement of boys.
- Although girls have overtaken boys in public examinations, some gender differences remain in subject choices. This is most apparent post-16 in science and technology.
- Colley (1998) found that despite the National Curriculum there are still significant gender differences remaining in option choices. She argues that this is affected by the students' perceptions of subjects.
- Today women outnumber men at university. They even dominate courses that were considered traditionally male such as medicine, dentistry, law, business and finance.

# Inside-school factors affecting the achievement of boys and girls

- State initiatives in the early 1980s were directed at the enhancement of girls' achievement. Examples include WISE (women into science and engineering), GIST (girls into science and technology) and some of the early Technical and Vocational Educational Initiative (TVEI) programmes.
- The increase in service-sector jobs has enhanced the employment opportunities for women.
- The women's movement and feminism may have influenced the aspirations of girls and the increasing independence of women may have filtered down into schools.
- The introduction of coursework was said to help girls as they had different study skills to boys. However, since 2009, coursework has been removed from many GCSE subjects. It is interesting to note that this has not reduced the achievement gap between girls and boys.
- The introduction of the National Curriculum ensured that girls could no longer drop out of traditionally masculine subjects like science and mathematics.
- Laddish behaviour in the classroom and the more general anti-learning, anti-school attitudes of teenage boys has been seen as a means of off-setting generally poor levels of esteem they get from staff and girls (Francis 2000).

> **Knowledge check 11**
>
> Suggest three effects of the National Curriculum on girls' achievement.

# Outside-school factors affecting males and females

- Changes in attitudes: the introduction of a laddish culture (including magazines for young men and the rise of football chat-shows on television) in the 1990s, which viewed schoolwork as 'uncool'.
- Changes in the labour market: an increase in unemployment for young men, together with the decline of traditional manufacturing industries. The situation is especially acute for white working-class boys. In 2007 these boys accounted for almost half of students leaving school with low qualifications or with no exam passes at all.

**Educational underachievement**
Not achieving success to the level of one's ability.

- Changes in the family, such as increased divorce and lone-parenting, have led to a lack of effective role models for many boys and encouraged the idea of economic independence for young women.
- Gender issues are affected by class and ethnicity too, as some social groups — especially Chinese, African and middle-class Asian girls — achieve much higher standards than others.

## Key concepts

femininity/masculinity; feminism; gender socialisation; laddism; malestream; nature vs nurture; patriarchy; sexism

## Key thinkers

Sharpe, Stanworth, Deem, Spender, Kelly, Delamont, Rutherford, Mac an Ghaill

# Ethnicity

While it is true that some ethnic minorities underachieve in the British education system, it is a mistaken generalisation to argue that this is true of all ethnic minorities. The highest achievers in terms of educational qualifications are students from Indian and Chinese backgrounds and Asian students from East African backgrounds. Although the performance of black Caribbean and Pakistani and Bangladeshi students has improved considerably over the past decade, boys from these ethnic groups still underachieve. (It is important to remember that it is white working-class boys who are the lowest achievers at present.)

Several factors affect the achievement of minority ethnic groups.

## Inside-school explanations

### Curriculum bias and ethnocentrism

Subjects such as English literature, history and religious education have been accused of being ethnocentric. The foci of these subjects have tended to be the achievements of white European (Christian) peoples. The National Curriculum has marginalised the history of black people, and foreign languages taught in school remain primarily European. Where other languages are taught these tend to be extra-curricular.

### Teacher expectations

Recent research has indicated that teachers have lower expectations of black boys than they have of other pupils. These pupils tend to be stereotyped as troublemakers and seen as disruptive. Some sociologists would argue that this labelling is likely to result in a self-fulfilling prophecy.

## Institutional racism

In 1999, Ofsted published a damning report on British education, claiming that there was institutional racism within the system. This claim echoed earlier criticisms expressed in the 1985 Swann Report, which claimed that unintentional racism was a feature of many schools. In the 1970s Bernard Coard argued that the British education system made black Caribbean pupils 'educationally subnormal'. He argued that the system diminished the self-esteem of black Caribbean children. As Blair et al. show (2003), there is a marked lack of black role models in British schools. Sociologists have also pointed to the lack of ethnic minority head teachers. Recent sociological evidence confirms that many ethnic minority students receive more negative criticism and stereotyping from staff than do white students whether intentional or not.

## Pupil exclusions

Pupil exclusions have risen markedly since the 1980s. This may be due to the focus on league tables and the reduction in specialist support for pupils with behavioural and learning difficulties. However, Afro-Caribbean pupils are significantly over-represented in exclusion figures. Explanations focus on teacher attitudes, for example seeing black pupils as more disruptive, and on black pupils expressing their frustration in the classroom at the effects of poverty and racism.

**Knowledge check 12**

Explain 'institutional racism'.

# Outside-school explanations

## Racism

It is impossible to isolate racism in the school from the experience of living in a racist society. All pupils from black, Asian and refugee backgrounds face the threat of racial abuse and attack in Britain. Victimisation studies indicate that Asians are 50 times more likely to be the victims of a racist attack than white people, while black people are 36 times more likely to be victims.

## Home factors and parental interest

Cultural deprivation models have placed the blame for educational underachievement on the home. Afro-Caribbean home life has been stereotyped as more stressful, with higher proportions of lone parents and lower family incomes. Pryce claimed that family life among West Indians in Bristol was 'turbulent'. In contrast, Asian families are seen to be a positive resource for their children, with greater emphasis on educational success.

## Language factors

In the past, language factors were seen to be significant constraints for both Afro-Caribbean and Asian pupils. It was claimed that pupils coming from homes where English was not the first language were disadvantaged. However, Driver and Ballard rejected this explanation and the Swann Report did not emphasise this view.

## Social class

There are marked socioeconomic differences between ethnic minorities in Britain. As far back as 1985, the Swann Report identified socioeconomic factors as being important in the underachievement of children from Afro-Caribbean backgrounds. In 2007 boys from these backgrounds still fared worse educationally than Afro-Caribbean girls and white students. It is probable that the growing number of violent youth gangs on lower socioeconomic estates may have a significant impact on the educational success of these boys.

# Criticisms/racism reconsidered

Fuller's research showed that black girls did not accept negative teacher expectations and they fought the labels to achieve success. Stone's research questioned the view that black pupils have low self-esteem. Many pupils in the study were hostile to teachers yet maintained a positive self-image. Prejudice among teachers might be expressed in the staff room but might not necessarily extend into the classroom.

## Key concepts

labelling and the self-fulfilling prophecy; ethnocentrism; institutional racism; resistance; curriculum bias

## Key thinkers

Wright, Coard, Fuller, Mirza, Pilkington, Brittan, Driver and Ballard, Pryce, Mac an Ghaill

---

**Summary**

After studying this section you should be able to explain:
- the differential educational achievement of social groups by social class, gender and ethnicity in terms of inside- and outside-school factors

- inside-school factors including labelling, setting and streaming, the curriculum (both official and hidden)
- outside factors including material deprivation, cultural deprivation, language speech codes, racism and sexism

# Relationships and processes in schools (teacher/pupil relationships; pupil subcultures; the hidden curriculum and the organisation of teaching and learning)

## Teacher/pupil relationships

### Key ideas

- Labelling.
- Self-fulfilling prophecy.
- Teacher expectations — linked to:
  - social class
  - gender
  - ethnicity

(These are all discussed earlier in the guide.)

## Pupil subcultures

### Key ideas

- Subcultures are created through processes within the school such as streaming and labelling.
- Some teachers label lower-stream students as 'failures'. The students attempt to protect their self-identity and self-worth by forming subcultures. Understanding the development of subcultures tends to come from the interactionist approach.
- Early theorists like Cohen and Miller explained the creation of subcultures as resulting from status frustration and the focal concerns of working-class boys. It was assumed that as they were unlikely to be successful within the education system, they would find status outside the classroom.
- Woods and other researchers have argued that pupils' adaptations to the experience of school life depend on acceptance or rejection of the importance of academic success. Woods has identified eight adaptations: ingratiation, compliance, opportunism, ritualism, retreatism, colonisation, intransigence and rebellion. He has related these adaptations to social class by arguing that middle-class students tend to have the more

**Status frustration**
The anger experienced by working-day boys as a result of unemployment and lack of social prestige.

conformist adaptations, whereas working-class pupils show the least conformist adaptations.

## Resistance and failure

Willis, from a Marxist perspective, identified two subcultures: the 'lads' and the 'ear'oles'. The lads did not value education and qualifications but felt themselves to be superior to the ear'oles who were compliant in school in order to gain skilled employment later. Although the lads claimed to resist and 'have a laff at' the system, ironically it was preparing them for low-skilled manual work.

## Resistance and success

Fuller's study of a group of Afro-Caribbean girls in a London comprehensive demonstrated another form of resistance. The girls, labelled as failures by their teacher, rejected the negative label and worked hard to ensure their success. Fuller's work is important in showing that subcultural resistance does not necessarily mean academic failure.

### Evaluation

+ Draws attention to the importance of peer groups and subcultures.
+ Gives another aspect of the influence of in-school factors on underachievement.
– Takes a relatively deterministic approach to the development of subcultures. It is possible that at times even the more conformist pupils will become deviant and disruptive if teachers are seen to be lacking classroom discipline.
– Not all teachers adopt a middle-class view of the world and might be more sympathetic to the anti-authoritarianism of some pupils.

### Key concepts

delinquent subcultures; labelling; resistance; self-fulfilling prophecy; streaming

### Key thinkers

Hargreaves, Woods, Willis, Fuller, Mac an Ghaill, Rist

# Hidden curriculum

## Key ideas

● This is a Marxist concept that focuses on internal processes within the school that do not form part of the official or overt curriculum. These processes are seen as mirroring the outside capitalist society.

> **Examiner tip**
> It is important to remember that not all pupils accept the labels that teachers give them. Some pupils consciously reject these labels because they do not accept the authority of those teachers. This resistance may result in academic success.

- They include values, attitudes and beliefs that are passed on through the socialisation process within schooling.
- The **correspondence principle** shows the links between school and work.

## Key concepts

correspondence principle; fragmentation; extrinsic rewards

## Key thinkers

Bowles and Gintis

**Correspondence principle** Processes in schools replicate those in the workplace. As well as punctuality and obedience to authority, middle-class children are prepared for more managerial occupations.

# The organisation of teaching and learning

## Key ideas

- Social policies relating to education emphasise teaching and learning rather than just teaching.
- Teaching and learning styles: the emphasis in education changed from the process of teachers teaching students to one where students' learning processes became prominent. This emphasised the different ways in which individuals learn, including multiple intelligences, personalised learning and the use and impact of new technologies in the classroom.
- Switching-on: successful pupils learn how to please the teacher.
- Switching-off: pupils fail to conform to teachers' expectations and do not value what is being taught.

## Key thinkers

Cano-Garcia and Hughes, Barrett

After studying this section, you should be able to explain the processes that occur within school, including:
- teacher/pupil relationships
- pupil subcultures
- the hidden curriculum
- the organisation of teaching and learning

**Summary**

# Educational policies (including selection, comprehensivisation and marketisation)

## 1870 Education Act

The 1870 Forster Act introduced elementary education for all 5- to 10-year-olds. By 1880 it was compulsory for all children to be educated to the age of 10. A limited curriculum was offered focusing on the importance of the 'four Rs': reading, writing, arithmetic and religion.

Over the twentieth century the school leaving age was gradually raised to 16 years. However, social class and education were clearly linked. Until the Second World War, there were three broad types of school, according to social class:

- elementary schools for the working class
- grammar schools for the middle classes (these were fee-paying institutions)
- public schools for the upper classes

**Examiner tip**
Although you will not be expected to know the history of the education system in great detail, you will be expected to have some idea of the main changes that have taken place over the last century, as a result of government policies.

## 1944 Education Act

The 1944 Butler Act, a fundamental part of the creation of the welfare state, introduced free state education for all pupils in England and Wales from 5 to 15 years. The aim of the Act was to provide equality of educational opportunity for all children, regardless of their socioeconomic background. The Act introduced the tripartite system whereby all state pupils took an examination at 11. On the basis of this test, pupils were allocated to one of three types of secondary school: grammar, secondary modern or technical.

### Grammar schools

These schools were intended for the academically able and were modelled on the public schools. Only 20% of the school population attended grammar school and their intake was predominantly middle class. Pupils had to pass the 11-plus examination to attend.

### Secondary modern schools

Approximately 75% of children attended this type of school, which offered a basic education and little opportunity to take external exams. Approximately 80% of secondary modern pupils left without any qualifications.

# Technical schools

These schools emphasised vocational subjects and technical skills. There were very few technical schools built and they were attended by only 5% of the school population.

# Criticisms of the tripartite system

## Parity of esteem

The tripartite system was founded on the idea of separate but equal types of school for the different aptitudes and abilities of students. However, in reality grammar schools were afforded much higher status than secondary modern and technical schools. Few technical schools were built and the system was really bipartite rather than tripartite.

**Knowledge check 13**

Explain 'parity of esteem'.

## Low self-esteem

The system resulted in educational success or failure at age 11. Failing the 11-plus created low self-esteem in children and turned them off schooling at an early age. The 11-plus system was responsible for a huge wastage of educational talent, since the majority of secondary modern students left school with no qualifications. Sociologists critical of the validity of IQ tests believe that they are not valid indicators of intelligence but are culturally biased and ethnocentric.

## Social class

Although the system was designed to remove class barriers to education, in reality there was a very strong correlation between social class and secondary school. Grammar schools were for the most part middle-class institutions, leaving working-class children to a second-rate education in a secondary modern.

**Examiner tip**

It is important to remember that in Britain today, many children sit entrance exams for increasing numbers of selective primary and secondary schools. Therefore these criticisms are still relevant to our current education system.

# Comprehensivisation

By the 1960s, concerns were being raised that the tripartite system had not achieved its aim to democratise education and end the class system. The aim of the tripartite system to produce a meritocracy had failed. In response, the Labour government proposed the introduction of comprehensive schools, designed to introduce more social mixing and eradicate testing at 11. In 1965, the Labour government required all local education authorities (LEAs) to submit plans to show how they would become comprehensive. This was a very slow business and one that was opposed by the Conservatives. However, by 1974, 80% of secondary pupils attended a comprehensive school.

# Criticisms of comprehensivisation

- Standards have been lowered and higher-ability children have been held back.
- Comprehensivisation has not succeeded in more social mixing, as class differences persist in terms of educational attainment and staying on rates post-16.
- Comprehensives have also failed to produce a meritocracy.

- Schools in middle-class areas tend to have much higher pass rates than those in working-class areas.
- The 1990s saw further attacks on state schooling by Ofsted. Schools were assessed according to strict guidelines and some were seen as not meeting the various criteria for success. The language and systems of the business world entered education and this came to be known as the 'marketisation of education'.

**Marketisation of education** The process whereby the education system is understood in business terms: target setting, competition and consumer choice.

## Responses to the criticisms

- Educational pass rates have risen significantly since the 1960s. Today many more children leave school with qualifications than did in the tripartite system.
- Evidence suggests that children of the highest academic ability do as well in comprehensives as in other types of state school.
- The state system has always had to compete with private schools and grammar schools. In many areas, private and grammar schools have 'creamed off' the brightest children, while the assisted-places scheme introduced by the Conservatives in 1980 allowed less affluent 'gifted' children to attend a private school without having to pay the fees. Even here the assisted places went overwhelmingly to middle-class children.

# 1988 Education Reform Act

The 1988 Education Reform Act has had the most significant impact on schooling since 1944. It introduced a set of far-reaching reforms on education.

## National Curriculum

For the first time in Britain the government decided which subjects should be studied in all state schools. English, Maths and Science became core subjects for all 11- to 16-year-olds and it also became compulsory for all secondary school students to study a foreign language.

## Parental choice

The Act encouraged parents to choose a secondary school for their child. Critics argue that, in reality, this choice only increased the social divisions in schools and allowed middle-class parents to play the system to their advantage.

## National testing (SATs)

With the aim of raising national standards, testing and national attainment targets were introduced for children at ages 7, 11, 14 and 16.

## Local management of schools (LMS)

The Act changed the nature of funding for schools. LMS meant that each school had more power over its budget. The responsibility for managing the budget was removed from the LEA and given to the head teacher and the governors.

# New Labour and educational policy

Between 1997 and 2010, the 'New' Labour government emphasised the links between education and work. Its policies have been referred to as post-Fordist in that they focused on education in a global market, and viewed education and training as crucial for economic success. Its policies included the following:

- encouragement of nursery education
- literacy and numeracy hours in primary schools and the setting up of the National Literacy Strategy
- reduction of class sizes to 30 in primary schools
- home–school contracts
- target setting
- Ofsted inspection of schools, including naming and shaming 'failing schools' and direct intervention in such schools by government agencies
- setting up of the Learning and Skills Council (2000) to oversee post-16 education and training in order to improve standards
- setting up education action zones (EAZ) from 1998 together with social exclusion units to tackle problems emerging from areas of high social deprivation (including Sure Start initiatives)
- the New Deal to get the young unemployed and lone parents back to work
- the expansion of specialist schools as 'centres of excellence' in specific subject areas such as arts and media, sports, technology and business
- encouragement of faith schools — usually established by a single faith group
- Curriculum 2000: introduction of AS and A2 rather than a single A-level examination
- Education Maintenance Allowance for 16-year-olds in full-time education
- the setting up of City Academies funded by the state and private enterprise
- social inclusion: vocational education and work experience for disaffected school students, Excellence in Cities, Sure Start, Extended Schools, New Start
- Tomlinson Report (2004) and the introduction of the 14 to 19 Diploma

**Examiner tip**
Find out which (if any) of these policies no longer exist.

## Evaluation

+ New Labour built many new schools in very deprived areas and put in place the building schools for the future programme (BSF).
+ Policies such as EAZs and the reduction of class sizes helped to reduce inequality.
+ Trowler (2003) maintained that educational funding increased significantly; resources for deprived areas were enhanced; an emphasis on lifelong learning enabled those who hadn't achieved at school to realise their potential.
- Marxists criticise New Labour for not reducing inequality of opportunity but increasing social class divisions through parental choice.
- The introduction of tuition fees for higher education students affected the economically underprivileged disproportionately.

- Some critics maintain that increasing examination success is a result of exams being 'dumbed down'.
- Whitty (2002) criticised reforms such as parental choice for allowing the middle class to benefit rather than producing a more egalitarian system.
- New Labour wrongly assumed that the education system is capable of solving most social problems and promoting social change.

**Examiner tip**

Exam questions on educational policies could range from short questions to a 20-mark essay.

**Examiner tip**

It is important to keep up to date with educational policies. For example, the rules have now changed so that any school can apply for academy status.

# Conservative/Liberal Democrat coalition government (2010)

- The introduction of free schools.
- University tuition fees increased to up to £9,000 per year.
- English Baccalaureate for state schools.
- Increase in academies, but not specifically designated for deprived areas.
- Schools with an OFSTED judgement of 'outstanding' may opt out of local authority control and become academies.
- So far, considerable criticism has been levelled at the coalition, but these changes to the education system have not been in place long enough to be reviewed.
- The increased involvement of the private sector in education.

**Summary**

After studying this section you should have an understanding of the structure, role, impact and experience of education and be able to explain the significance of educational policies, including:

- selection
- comprehensivisation
- marketisation

# Sociological research methods

## Positivist and interpretivist approaches to research

### Positivism

Positivists assume that sociological explanations should be like those of the natural sciences, and that sociologists should use the logic, methods and procedures of natural science.

## Key ideas

- Social reality can be measured objectively by using scientific methods.
- As with the natural world, social behaviour is governed by underlying **causal laws** and can, therefore, be predicted.
- By systematic observation of causal relationships between social phenomena, these laws can be revealed. (An example of the discovery of causal laws can be seen in Durkheim's work on suicide, where he showed that social laws affected an individual's likelihood of suicide.)

**Causal laws** These are hard to identify in sociology as they are unseen. They are generated by events and relationships which underpin social action.

### Evaluation

- + As far as possible, scientists and sociologists must be personally objective in their research. The data would then be reliable and would not be dependent on the subjectivity of the researcher.
- + Positivists rely on empirical evidence in testing their assumptions. They argue that assuming what people are thinking is both impossible and inappropriate to scientific research.
- − Positivism fails to understand that individuals create social reality through their interactions.
- − It assumes that there is only one view of social reality.
- − It does not allow us to see the world from the position of the social actor.

**Knowledge check 14**

(a) Explain the difference between theoretical and empirical.

(b) What do interpretivists mean by the term 'social actor'?

# Interpretivism

Interpretivism rejects the idea that social behaviour can be studied using the same methodology as that of natural science. Interpretivists do not accept that there is a single social reality but see many realities produced through interactions of individuals. Weber's *verstehen* sociology emphasised that sociologists had to interpret the meanings of social action as understood by the social actors involved. Sociologists needed to put themselves in the position of the person or group being observed.

## Key ideas

- The subject matter of sociology is fundamentally different from that of the natural sciences.
- The subjective consciousness of individuals is not measurable.
- There is no possibility of gaining understanding of social action through scientific methods.
- Social meanings are the most important aspect of interaction and these need to be understood by sociologists using qualitative methods.
- There are no causal laws governing social behaviour.

## Sociological approaches

Phenomenology, social action, symbolic interactionism, feminism, *verstehen* sociology

### Evaluation

+ Interpretivism allows us to see that individuals perceive social reality in different ways.
+ Individuals are not passive — they are not seen as simply manipulated by external forces but as active individuals, making choices and acting on social meanings.
- Methods used tend to rely on the subjectivity of the researcher.
- It fails to examine the effects of power differences on social interaction.
- It underestimates the extent and impact of social structure on individuals.

**Knowledge check 15**

What is the difference between objectivity and subjectivity?

## Links to methods

These approaches are linked with specific types of methods in research.

**Positivist** sociologists see social reality as objective and measurable and favour quantitative methods, such as social surveys using postal or self-administered questionnaires and/or structured interviews. They sometimes, but rarely, undertake laboratory experiments and also make use of official statistics as secondary data. Content analysis of the media is usually quantitative.

**Interpretivist** sociologists see social reality as constructed by social actors through the meanings of social action. They tend to favour qualitative methods such as covert and overt participant observation, unstructured or semi-structured interviews and field experiments. Secondary data sources are more likely to be personal documents and descriptive historical documents, and also oral histories and self-report studies. Content analysis of the media is qualitative and thematic, and semiology may sometimes be used.

However, many sociologists are increasingly making use of methodological pluralism, which is using more than one method in one research project. This enhances validity, reliability and generalisability.

# Methods of sociological research

**Quantitative methods**
These produce numerical and statistical data.

**Qualitative methods**
These produce rich, in-depth, meaningful data.

Methods can be quantitative or qualitative. They can also be divided into **primary** methods of data collection, where researchers collect the data themselves, and **secondary** methods, where the data have been collected by another (or others) for a purpose other than the present research. Primary and secondary data can be both quantitative and qualitative.

**Primary data** are collected through **social surveys** using questionnaires and/or interviews; **experiments** including laboratory and field, or by use of the **comparative method** if experiment is not possible; **observation**, including non-participant and participant observation.

**Secondary data** can take the form of quantitative evidence such as **Official Statistics** or more qualitative evidence such as **personal documents**, for example letters, diaries, photographs, and **historical documents** such as parish records.

It is also possible for previous research produced by other sociologists to be used as secondary data. **Content analysis** of mass media material can be both quantitative and qualitative.

In the AS examination, you will be required to answer free-standing questions on research methods as well as questions on research methods used in the context of educational research. This section includes some examples of studies from educational research that you can use in answering questions on methods in an educational context, as well as examples of studies from other substantive areas of sociology.

# Primary research methods

## Operationalising concepts

Before researchers choose the research method(s) for their study, they need to operationalise the concepts that they are going to research. This means that they must 'translate' the concept into something that can be measured. For example, Blauner, in researching the concept of alienation, divided it into distinct aspects: meaninglessness, powerlessness, normlessness, isolation and self-estrangement.

## Sampling techniques

For most sociological studies, the research or target population is too large. Consequently, the researcher has to find an appropriate but smaller group of individuals to study. This smaller group is called a sample. There are many different ways in which samples can be selected. It is important to note that the type of sample and the way in which it is chosen may have important consequences for the reliability of the data collected, but first some concepts:

- **research or target population:** the whole group being studied, e.g. all year 10 pupils in one school
- **sampling frame:** the list (if one exists) of names of the entire research population
- **sampling unit:** one individual person or institution taken from the sampling frame

There are several different kinds of sampling procedures, some of which are more representative than others:

- **Representative sampling**: the social characteristics of the sample must resemble those of the research population in, as far as possible, the exact proportion that they occur in that population. So, for example, a sample by gender of a school must have the same proportion of boys and girls as there is in that school.
- **Random sampling**: in a random sample each person or unit has an equal chance of being selected. At its simplest it is a 'picking out of a hat' method. More sophisticated techniques involve random number tables. Simple random sampling will rarely produce representative samples — for instance, randomly choosing a sample of schoolchildren is very unlikely to produce numbers of girls and boys in the same proportion as exists in the school.
- **Stratified random sampling**: this technique is more representative as it divides the research population into specific groups or strata (e.g. all the boys in a school in one group and all the girls in another) and then a sample from each group is randomly selected in the same proportion as they appear in the population.

**Knowledge check 16**

Explain the difference between primary and secondary data.

- **Quota sampling**: this is the usual method used for market research and opinion polls. An interviewer is given a quota of interviews to conduct with individuals fulfilling specific characteristics, e.g. sex, age, social class. The sample is not random, as the choice of interviewees lies with the interviewer. Individuals with the same social characteristics do not have an equal chance of being selected.
- **Multistage samples**: this provides a cheaper and quicker alternative to actual random samples. It involves different stages, at each of which the samples are subdivided. It may be used for opinion polls for example, where constituencies are chosen and then samples are drawn from them.
- **Snowball sampling**: this is used only in cases where there is no sampling frame. The researcher finds subjects through personal contacts. It is particularly useful when sampling deviant groups, where initial contact with one person can generate further contacts, who can then bring in yet more people.
- **Volunteer sampling**: this is similar to snowball sampling, but the researcher may use advertising or leaflets to find contacts. Milgram did this for his obedience to authority experiments.

**Examiner tip**
Short questions on the exam paper often require you to define/explain sampling techniques. Make sure you know several.

Each sampling technique has its advantages and disadvantages. So much depends on the nature of the research as to which one the researcher chooses.

## Social surveys

Social surveys are the most popular social research method because they can gather a great deal of data from a large section of the population in a relatively short space of time. They most frequently use pre-coded questionnaires; however, some social surveys can also be carried out through interviews.

Ackroyd and Hughes (1981) distinguish between three types of survey:

- factual — the government Census is a factual survey as it collects descriptive data
- attitude — opinion polls come into this category as they collect people's attitudes to events and issues
  - explanatory — these are more sociological as they are used to test hypotheses and produce new theories

## Questionnaires

A questionnaire is a pre-set, pre-coded list of standardised questions given to a respondent. If an interviewer reads out the questionnaire, it becomes a structured interview (see below). **Postal** questionnaires are mailed to respondents, usually with a stamped addressed envelope or some small incentive to return the form. **Online** questionnaires have become very popular with marketing companies and political lobbyists.

Questionnaires produce a large amount of quantitative data and can be given to a widespread target population. For example, the Census is given to every household in the country.

Questions can be open-ended, which gives the respondents an opportunity to expand on their answers, or, more usually, closed/fixed-choice questions where the respondents have limited choices.

## Evaluation

+ Positivist researchers see the data collected as being highly reliable and objective.
+ There is little personal involvement on the part of the researcher after the initial construction of the questionnaire, thus reducing the risk of researcher bias.
+ Large quantities of data can be produced, and quickly and easily analysed by computer.
+ Data can be used to test hypotheses, indicate social trends and make predictions of future trends.
+ Surveys are regarded as scientific by government agencies and opinion pollsters.
+ Postal and/or online questionnaires can be sent to a sample over a wide geographical area.
− The 'imposition problem'.
− Questionnaires are not appropriate if we want to find the meanings of and motivations for social behaviour.
− Different answers may not actually reflect real differences, as respondents may be interpreting questions in different ways.
− They can be too inflexible, as responses are limited.
− Language complexity.
− Operationalising concepts inevitably involves researcher bias.
− Validity may be low.
− Postal and internet questionnaires: low response rate, and a lack of representativeness.
− With qualitative data second order constructs are necessary.

**Second order constructs** These are the categories imposed by the researcher when generating meaning from the data (e.g. satisfaction with work).

Studies using questionnaires:

- **Shere Hite** (1988) sent out postal questionnaires to 100,000 women in the USA to question them on their sexual behaviour. Her book is based on 4,500 replies. This low response rate means that these replies cannot be taken as representative of the views of all American women.

### Questionnaires for educational research

**Ofsted (2007)** conducted a survey of lifestyles of more than 110,000 pupils aged 10–15 years. The issues included children's fears, their attitudes to schooling, bullying, alcohol consumption, and their hopes and aspirations. The survey was completed online at participating schools.

## Interviews

Several different kinds of interview are used by sociologists: structured, semi-structured and unstructured interviews; group and focus interviews, face-to-face or phone interviews. Almost all interviews involve a face-to-face interaction between an interviewer and an interviewee. They range from highly formal to a relaxed conversation. The length of the interview also varies.

- **Structured interviews**: these are pre-coded questionnaires (using an interview schedule) where standardised closed questions are asked by the interviewer to all interviewees. The quantitative data produced are easily collated and analysed by means of a computer and displayed in statistical ways to analyse patterns and trends, and to make comparisons between groups.
- **Unstructured interviews**: in contrast to the above, unstructured interviews are in-depth and non-standardised. Rapport and trust can be built up over a longer period of time. This approach is flexible, as it uses open-ended questions and gives the interviewees more freedom to express their views. Interpretivist and feminist researchers often adopt this qualitative method because they argue that it is a more democratic means of gaining data.
- **Semi-structured interviews**: this approach combines the advantages of both structured and unstructured interviews. The researcher can access data from standardised questions and the interviewee is able to elaborate where necessary, thus producing both quantitative and qualitative data.
- **Group interviews:** these are usually semi- or unstructured interviews. They are often used in market research and are called 'focus groups' when used by political parties to gain public opinion. In school research, sometimes researchers will prefer to interview pupils in a group situation as the pupils may be more relaxed.

**Examiner tip**

When answering any essay question on interviews, always link the method to positivism or interpretivism.

## Evaluation

+ Validity is likely to be high with semi-structured and unstructured interviews whereas reliability is higher with structured interviews.
+ The response rate for all interviews is much higher than for postal or self-administered questionnaires.
+ Interviewers can explain misunderstandings to the interviewee and prompt where necessary.
+ Feminists argue that unstructured interviews enable researchers to develop a more equal relationship with their subjects. Oakley used this approach with women on the labour ward in her book *From Here to Maternity*.
+ Natural settings are more likely to put interviewees at ease and help to produce more valid findings.
- Interviewer bias: researcher characteristics such as gender, ethnicity, accent etc. will affect responses from the interviewee.
- Cost: interviews are likely to cost more than self-administered questionnaires and for this reason fewer are undertaken, making the results less representative.
- Artificiality: formal interviews are likely to reduce the validity of the data collected.
- Group interviews may only gain the views of the most self-confident members, as the others may be intimidated and avoid speaking.

Studies using interviews:

- Unstructured interviews: **Dobash and Dobash** (1980) *Violence Against Wives*. The study was based on unstructured interviews with 109 women who had reported domestic violence to the police. Dobash and Dobash argued that their approach was the most appropriate because the subject matter of the research was very sensitive. They wanted to validate the women's experiences and let women speak for themselves.
- Semi-structured interviews: **Charlotte Butler** (1995) 'Religion and gender: young women and Islam', Sociology Review, Vol. 4 No. 3. Butler conducted 30 semi-structured interviews with young Muslim women in Britain to discover their relationship with their faith.

## Interviews for educational research

- **Unstructured interviews**: **Labov (1973)** challenged the use of the formal interview when interviewing children. In his conversations with young black boys he found that they were more forthcoming if the interviews took place more informally.
- **Group interviews**: **Willis (1977)** studied a group of working-class boys during their last year in secondary school and their first year in work. As well as participant observation, he used group interviews (structured conversations) with the boys. This allowed him to observe interactions between the boys as they talked.
- **Ball, Bowe and Gewirtz (1994)** conducted a study of 15 schools in three LEAs to examine the possible effects that parental choice and the encouragement of competition between schools had on education and on differential opportunity. They used a variety of methods including attending meetings, examining documents, visiting schools, and interviews with head teachers, parents and teachers.

# Experiments: laboratory and field

The experiment is the classic research method of the natural sciences. It is the means by which hypotheses are empirically tested. Experiments involve the manipulation of an independent variable (cause) and the observation of a dependent variable (effect), while controlling extraneous variables in order to test a hypothesis.

**Hypothesis** A predictive statement that is a possible explanation of a particular phenomenon. It needs to be tested in order to be confirmed or not.

## Laboratory experiments

Laboratory experiments are designed to achieve a rigorous empirical test in which variables are closely controlled and observations and measurements are accurately recorded so that the effect of changing one or more of the variables can be analysed. By rigorous experimentation the researcher aims to identify cause and effect rather than simply a chance occurrence.

**Examiner tip**

The summer riots of 2011 in Britain can be understood as a natural experiment. Sociologists could investigate, for example, the effects of unemployment, poverty and cuts in welfare expenditure on youth in the inner cities.

## Natural experiments

These rely on chance occurrences and are often rare. The researcher may be able to check on the relationship between variables when such occasions happen.

## Evaluation

+ The experiment is internally valid if it has been conducted in a rigorous manner. It is then possible that the hypothesis has been proven, and cause and effect have been identified.
+ Although highly unethical, Milgram's experiment taught us a great deal about obedience to authority. Zimbardo's work showed the effects of prison and the guards' abuse of power.
- Experiments are rarely used for practical, theoretical and ethical reasons.
- Artificiality: a limited number of conditions can be simulated in a laboratory, making it impossible to recreate normal life.
- Demand characteristics and the experimenter effect: awareness of being in an experiment affects the behaviour of the subject.
- Ethics: short- and long-term effects and deception.

Studies using experiments:

- In the 'Obedience to Authority' experiment (1974), **Stanley Milgram** found that 65% of his 40 volunteers were willing to inflict apparently dangerous electric shocks of up to 450 volts on people when instructed to do so by individuals in authority.
- **Zimbardo**'s prison study demonstrated the negative effects of allowing students to role-play prisoners and wardens.
- In the 1930s **Mayo** et al. conducted a series of work-based experiments (the Hawthorne studies) that tested the effects of changing working conditions on worker productivity.

**Hawthorne effect**
When people are aware of being observed as part of a research study, their behaviour changes.

## Field experiments

Not all experiments on people are carried out in a laboratory. Field experiments test social behaviour in the real world in everyday social contexts. For example, a study of social class conducted at Paddington Station compared people's responses to a request for directions when a researcher wore a formal suit with responses to the same request when the same researcher wore workmen's clothes.

## Experiments for educational research

In a field experiment, **Rosenthal and Jacobson (1968)** used IQ tests to demonstrate the self-fulfilling prophecy in a primary school in California. Although now very dated, this study is still considered a classic example of teacher expectations. Many students believe this to be a participant observation study, however the researchers did not observe the classroom interactions but simply returned to the school after about a year and re-tested the pupils. Their study is considered to be highly unethical because they knowingly deceived teachers and were engaged in potential social engineering of the children in the study.

# Participant observation

Participant observation involves the researcher joining the group he/she wishes to study and observing social interaction in a natural context. Sometimes known as the 'ethnographic approach', participant observation is a research method commonly used by interpretivists. The researcher may observe the group with or without their knowledge.

Covert participant observation involves deception of a group, where the researcher uses a disguise or lies to the group in order to study them. With overt participant observation the group members are aware they are being studied and the researcher's identity is known. However, in many participant observation studies, the overt/covert line is not so clear cut because the researcher's identity may be known to some but not all of the group's members or the group may have some idea that the researcher is writing about the area/institution but not necessarily about them.

**Ethnography** The study of the way of life of a social group over a period of time. It usually relies on a variety of methods.

> **Examiner tip**
> Make it clear that you understand the difference between overt and covert participant observation.

## Evaluation

+ Interpretivists claim that participant observation produces highly valid data. Social actors are studied in a natural environment and the data are in-depth and detailed.
+ Unlike survey techniques the participant observer does not impose his/her definition of reality on those studied. Social actors are allowed to speak for themselves and the researcher's aim is to achieve *verstehen* — to see the world from the point of view of others.
+ Participant observation may be the only way to gain access to the group. This is likely to be the case with socially deviant groups who would not be identifiable using a traditional sampling frame.
+ Participant observation may provide answers to questions that the researcher had not even considered asking.
- Covert participant observation raises many ethical issues. The group has not given consent to being observed and their trust has been broken.
- Researchers can become over-involved with the group's activities, stop observing and simply take part. This is known as 'going native'.
- Positivists claim that participant observation is unreliable and unscientific. Participant observation studies are impossible to replicate in the same way as survey data.
- Participant observation is a highly individual technique and requires tremendous skill on the part of the researcher. This is particularly true of covert participant observation.
- Recording data is also difficult for covert researchers.
- Getting in, staying in and getting out of the group can be very difficult. The researcher is likely to rely on a disguise or story to gain entry to the group and may have to leave suddenly if he/she feels under threat. There is also the problem of 'role strain' in maintaining a false identity for any length of time.

Studies using participant observation:

- **Laud Humphreys** (1970) *Tearoom Trade*. Humphreys' aim was to investigate the world of impersonal gay sexual encounters in public toilets across the USA. Humphreys acted as a voyeur (look-out) for the men and repeated his observations across the USA. He wanted to discover the marital status of those men and identified them through their car registration numbers. Humphreys then visited them at home under the pretext of conducting a health survey.
- **James Patrick** (1973) *Glasgow Gang Observed*. Patrick covertly studied a gang of young men in Glasgow. He joined the gang on the invitation of one of its members but he was covert to the rest of the group and he changed his appearance to fit in. Patrick left the group in a hurry when their violence became too problematic and he delayed publication of the study for several years using a pseudonym.
- **Sallie Westwood** (1984) *All Day Every Day: Factory and Family in the Making of Women's Lives*. An overt participant observation study of women hosiery workers. Westwood observed and interviewed women at work and joined them for nights out on the town. She combined an ethnographic approach with a feminist analysis of marriage, relationships, family life and work.
- **Nigel Fielding** (1993) conducted covert observation of the National Front. He argued that he would not have gained access if he had been an overt observer.

**Knowledge check 17**

Give three ethical problems associated with covert participant observation.

## Case studies

A case study is 'a detailed in-depth study of one group or event. The group or event is not necessarily representative of others of its kind, and case studies are used as preliminary pieces of research to generate hypotheses for subsequent research' (Lawson and Garrod, 1996, *The Complete A to Z Sociology Handbook*). This approach is sometimes referred to as ethnographic.

A case study may involve research into a single institution such as a school or factory, a community or even a family. The aim of a case study is to gain a detailed understanding of the way of life of those observed. A sociologist may combine several methods in the case study but, in general, researchers tend to favour qualitative approaches such as participant observation and unstructured interviewing to gain an in-depth understanding of the group.

### Evaluation

+ Case studies provide the sociologist with detailed and valid data.
+ They may serve to challenge and disprove existing assumptions about social groups. For example, the work of Eileen Barker on the Moonies challenged media fears of brainwashing by the sect.
+ The research may act as a springboard for further research in the field.
− The group or institution under study may be atypical and therefore the results will not be generalisable.
− Case studies are often a highly individual technique and this raises the problem of subjectivity on the part of the researcher.
− The data collected may be valid but are not reliable.

Studies using the case study method:

- **Paul Willis**'s study *Learning to Labour* (1977) was based on 12 working-class lads and their experience of education and their first year at work.
- **Eileen Barker**'s research for *The Making of a Moonie* (1984) involved the use of surveys, unstructured interviews and participant observation over a number of years, examining recruitment patterns and the experience of life as a member of the sect.

# Secondary data

## Quantitative secondary data: official statistics

Official statistics are numerical data produced by both central and local government. They provide a rich source of information for sociologists.

Sociologists often differentiate between hard statistics and soft statistics. **Hard statistics** are those figures that are seen to be relatively immune to processes of manipulation and bias in their collection, e.g. birth, death, marriage and divorce statistics. Although divorce statistics may not be a particularly valid indicator of unhappiness in marriage in society, they are a completely reliable indicator of the number of divorces because you cannot legally terminate a marriage without becoming a statistic.

In contrast, **soft statistics** are those figures that are prone to subjectivity and manipulation in their collection and presentation. They include data on crime, poverty, unemployment and suicide — aspects of society about which people may make value judgements. It is possible to see that the collection and interpretation of such data may be politically motivated to benefit those in power.

### Evaluation

+ Official statistics are very useful for identifying trends and making comparisons over time and between countries.
+ A useful source of background data: they save the sociologist time and expense.
+ Positivists see official statistics as 'hard' objective and reliable data. The Census is conducted every 10 years and each household is bound by law to complete it, ensuring that the data collected are highly reliable and representative. This means that generalisations can be made about society.
- The data may not be exactly what the sociologist needs because they were collected for another purpose.
- Interpretivists question the validity of official statistics. They see them as socially constructed.
- Manipulation and bias: Marxists would argue that statistics produced by the state tend to reflect the interests of powerful elites. They may be used to justify the existing social order.
- Feminists argue that many statistics are sexist and reflect malestream research.

**Social construct** This is not naturally given, but the end product of a social process whereby a series of decisions have been made to produce it (e.g. an official statistic).

Studies using official statistics:

- **Durkheim** (1897) *Le Suicide*. An attempt to show that society could be studied in a rigorous and scientific manner. He used nineteenth-century European statistics on suicide and compared the rate between countries. He wanted to show that suicide was not simply an individual act but a social phenomenon.
- **Dobash and Dobash** (1980) *Violence Against Wives*. Dobash and Dobash used crime statistics as a starting point for their research into domestic violence against women in Scotland. From the interviews they conducted, they found that the official picture of domestic violence concealed a significant dark figure of crime.

### Official statistics for educational research

Official statistics in education, including league tables of individual schools' performance and educational qualifications by social class, gender, ethnic group etc., are invaluable for sociological research, but they are socially constructed.

## Qualitative secondary data

Sociologists often use secondary data in their research as background sources or they may analyse secondary data to test their own hypotheses. There are many kinds of secondary material available to the researcher that are qualitative, such as: letters, oral histories, diaries, biographies, autobiographies, novels, newspapers, and other media such as internet, radio, film, television and photography.

*Verstehen* The ability of the researcher to understand the social situation from the point of view of the social actors involved, as if the researcher might 'walk in their shoes'.

Interpretivist sociologists use life documents such as letters and diaries in research because individuals create these documents and reflect on their personal experiences or report their feelings about events in their lives. Interpretivist sociologists aim to achieve *verstehen* in their work and understand the meanings and motivations of social actors engaged in social action. Qualitative secondary material is in-depth, often expressive and meaningful. It should therefore enable researchers to gain a valid insight into the lives of those they wish to study.

### Evaluation

+ Qualitative secondary data can be invaluable sources of information about current and historical events.
+ They may provide detailed and valid accounts of people's thoughts and feelings at a particular time.
+ Secondary data may be the only possible way of understanding a group's way of life in the past.
+ Life documents offer a richer, more in-depth picture of the way people feel and act than is possible from social surveys and other quantitative approaches.
+ The data can be usefully combined with quantitative approaches to achieve more valid and reliable findings (methodological pluralism and triangulation).
– Life documents may be highly subjective and therefore biased and invalid.
– Autobiographies are inevitably selective and partial. They were written with an audience in mind and often aim to impress the reader. This is often the case with the autobiographies of politicians and celebrities.

– Historical documents may not cover the particular period desired or may be written from a particular political perspective.
– Positivists reject the use of these types of data because of a lack of reliability.
– As the data must be interpreted by the researcher, this inevitably introduces the element of subjectivity.

Studies using secondary qualitative data:

• **Thomas and Znaniecki** (1919) The Polish Peasant in Europe and America. The researchers made extensive use of a collection of documents including 764 letters, diaries and newspaper articles regarding immigration, and the arrival and lives of Polish émigrés in Europe and the USA.

### Secondary qualitative data for educational research

**Valery Hey** (1997) researched girls' friendships in two London comprehensive schools. Her study provides an interesting example of the effective use of secondary qualitative data. She combined overt participant observation with the use of notes scribbled in lessons and girls' diaries. The girls had kept their notes and letters for several years and were willing for Hey to use them. She claimed that the notes were an important means of transmitting the cultural values of friendship.

## Content analysis

Content analysis is the main research method used by media researchers. It can also be used to examine personal and historical documents. It is a systematic means of classifying and describing content of items in the press and on television. Content analysis can be both quantitative and qualitative.

**Quantitative content analysis** produces statistical data from a pre-coded coding schedule. A coding schedule is a document like a questionnaire and is completed for each newspaper article, television programme or magazine. It can be used to calculate the amount of space allocated to events and/or count the number of times a particular issue, group or even particular words occur.

**Qualitative content analysis** produces descriptive data and examines the messages and ideological content of the media or of particular documents. It can be used for example to look at the messages around gender or ethnic representation in the media by analysing photographs, dialogue, situations etc. This method often takes a semiological approach to texts.

### Evaluation

#### Quantitative

+ The material is easily available and inexpensive (even free).
+ The data are easily coded and analysed.
+ The method limits researcher effect as all coders follow the same schedule.

+ It can be used to monitor recent events and make comparisons over time.
- The problems of this method are similar to those of the questionnaire, as a coding schedule is used.
- Even though coders may be trained they may not code the material in the same way.
- Second-order constructs of the researcher may not reflect the way the audience receives the text.
- It does not address the issue of audience reception and may assume passivity.

### Qualitative

+ This method interrogates the meanings of texts and communications.
+ It can be used to interpret the underlying ideological messages of texts.
- Interpretation is a highly subjective process and individuals perceive things in different ways.
- Researchers rarely check out how the audience interprets the messages of the texts.
- Given the nature of the texts and forms of communication, the data are likely to be unrepresentative.

**Examiner tip**
You need to understand the reasons why researchers choose the particular method(s) for their research/study. An important guiding factor is their methodological perspective: that is, whether they are positivistic researchers or interpretivists, but practical and ethical considerations are also influential.

Studies using content analysis:

- **T. A. van Dijk** (1991) *Racism in the Press*. Van Dijk examined the coverage of race relations in the press by using both quantitative and qualitative content analysis.
- **The Glasgow Media Group** have used both quantitative and qualitative content analysis in many of their studies — from *Bad News* (1985) to *Message Received* (1999).
- This methodology has also been used to look at children's literature, especially focused on gender roles.

# Choice of methods (PET)

Sociologists face serious decisions when they engage in research. The most important one is which method(s) to choose, but this decision is also affected by many other factors. We can divide the factors that affect choice into three: practical, ethical and theoretical considerations (PET). Whichever factor is most significant depends upon the nature of the research.

## Practical decisions

- **Funding:** this may be **the most significant issue** for any researcher. So much in research depends on the availability of money — the size of the sample, the time available for the research, the number of research assistants etc. A lone researcher may carry out a study involving participant observation where there is likely to be no external funding, but a research department may be dependent on government funding for a large social survey. Funding bodies may have ownership rights over the research data and they may have power of veto on whether the research findings can be published. Some methods are more costly than others. For example, a survey using interviews is more expensive than one done with postal questionnaires. Similarly, unstructured interviews are more costly than structured interviews, as interviewers need specialised training; it takes longer and the data are not easily coded.

- **Time:** this is related to cost and can affect whether several interviews can take place over a period of time or if only one interview is possible.
- **Access:** without acceptance into the institution or group to be studied there will be no research. Researchers may be asked to take on a role in return for access. (For example, Willis helped with the youth wing of the school while doing his research for *Learning to Labour.*)
- **Danger:** the researcher may be placed at risk of personal harm by certain covert activities.
- **Opportunity:** the researcher needs to have research opportunities in order to undertake the research programme. Often this relies on permission being granted from those in positions of authority, such as school head teachers.

# Ethical decisions

- **Moral issues:** sociologists must follow the BSA ethical guidelines. They must also be aware of the sensitivity of some areas and the possible impact of their research on respondents. Research is not usually a two-way process and respondents may feel that their trust and friendship has been betrayed. In using covert observation of any kind, the subjects are always deceived, but the researcher may be able to debrief them after the research has ended.
- **Illegality:** researchers may be called upon to engage in criminal acts or to witness others doing so. This poses the problem of whether the researcher will report this activity to the appropriate agencies.
- **Danger:** in some cases researchers may place their subjects in danger during their study.
- **After-effects:** some methods such as experimentation may have short-term or more lasting effects on respondents who might not have been informed about the true nature and aim of the study.
- **Informed consent:** the researcher should try to conduct the research with the consent of the subjects. This gives them the opportunity to refuse to participate or to withdraw at any time.

> **Examiner tip**
> Every method raises ethical issues, whether they relate to sensitivity, informed consent, deception or harm to participants.

# Theoretical decisions

- The methodological approach of the researcher will also affect the choice of method. Positivistic researchers generally choose quantitative methods, while interpretivist and feminist researchers generally choose qualitative methods.
- The theoretical perspective of the researcher — whether he/she is Marxist, interpretivist, feminist etc. — will affect choice of method and the nature of the research.
- However, there are instances when the researcher will have to use a method that is chosen by the funding body. For example, large-scale, government-funded research will usually be quantitative.

# The application of research methods to the study of education

Sociologists studying the topic of education will choose methods that they find most appropriate and this, in effect, means that all sociological research methods are available to them. The choice of method depends on practical, ethical and theoretical factors, including the topics and issues to be investigated and the individuals to be researched.

One practical issue with researching children is that younger children are less likely to be able to complete lengthy questionnaires. Older children with literacy difficulties will also find this method a problem.

An important ethical issue is that of informed consent. Researchers must gain consent not only from the school, but also from parents and guardians. It is also extremely important to ensure that children are not harmed or disadvantaged in any way as a result of being part of the research. Earlier research such as that undertaken by Rosenthal and Jacobson, 'Pygmalion in the classroom' would not be ethically acceptable to researchers today. It could be seen as a form of social engineering, whereby some children were advantaged and some disadvantaged as a result of being part of the research process.

**Summary**

After studying this section you should be able to explain:

- quantitative and qualitative methods of research; their strengths and limitations; research design
- sources of data, including questionnaires, interviews, participant and non-participant observation, experiments, documents, and official statistics; the strengths and limitations of these sources

- the distinction between primary and secondary data, and between quantitative and qualitative data
- the relationship between positivism, interpretivism and sociological methods; the nature of 'social facts'
- the theoretical, practical and ethical considerations influencing choice of topic, choice of method(s) and the conduct of research

# Questions & Answers

## How to use this section

This section of the guide contains four papers of questions on **Education and Sociological Methods** in the style of the AQA exam. Each question is followed by a brief analysis of what to watch out for when answering it (shown by the icon ⓔ). The first three papers include both C-grade and A-grade responses to each question, with examiner's comments (preceded by the icon ⓔ). The A-grade responses are not 'model answers'. They are not the only, or even the best, way of answering these questions. It would be quite possible in the essay-type questions to take a different approach, to use different material or even to come to a different conclusion, and still gain very high marks. The C-grade responses may be on the right track but fail, for various reasons, to score as many marks. A fourth paper is provided without students' responses, but with examiner's advice. This is for you to answer yourself.

## Examinable skills

Assessment objectives 1 and 2 (AO1 and AO2) are an integral part of the AS specification, and each counts for approximately half of the available marks.

## Assessment objective 1 (AO1): knowledge and understanding

Knowledge and understanding are linked, therefore you must not only demonstrate possession of sociological knowledge but also be able to use it in a meaningful way. Understanding implies that you can select appropriate knowledge and use it in answer to a specific question. Knowledge and understanding includes the nature of sociological thought, methods of sociological enquiry and the two core themes: socialisation, culture and identity; and social differentiation, power and stratification. You also need to show your familiarity with a range of methods and sources of data, together with your understanding of the relationship between theory and methods.

## Assessment objective 2 (AO2): application, analysis, interpretation and evaluation

These skills relate to the acquisition and production of evidence, the interpretation of evidence and arguments, the presentation of evidence and arguments and their application to sociological debates. (Evidence includes primary and secondary sources and quantitative and qualitative data.)

You must show that you can analyse and evaluate the **design** of sociological investigations and the **method(s)** used in these investigations to collect and record evidence.

Unit 2 incorporates research methods in the context of education. You must understand how research evidence has been gained and what methods have been used to produce the evidence. You will need to apply, interpret, and analyse the research methods and data and evaluate methods, sources and evidence.

**Examiner tip**

Sometimes a question will make a specific reference to an item, such as 'With reference to Item A', or 'Using material from Item B and elsewhere'. Always follow the instruction. One way to do this is to say:

*'The view referred to in Item A is that...'*

Or *'Item B shows evidence of...'*

**Examiner tip**

Before you move on to the questions and answers, read the next section carefully as it will help you to answer the 'Methods in Context' questions.

# The unit test

Education is examined together with Sociological Methods. The unit exam paper is allocated 2 hours and contains nine questions.

- Questions 01 to 04 are on Education and are awarded 40 marks in total.
- Question 05 refers to sociological research methods in the context of education. This is a one-part question and is awarded 20 marks.
- Questions 06 to 09 refer to freestanding research methods. These four questions are awarded 30 marks in total.

The marks for the paper total 90. The unit is worth 60% of the AS qualification and 30% of the total A-level qualification.

Questions **04** and **05** on the examination paper feature source material — one item per question. These will help you by giving useful information for your answer. It is important that you read the items carefully, and refer to them in your answer.

## Methods in context question (05): applying your knowledge and understanding of sociological research methods to the study of a particular issue in education

This question tests your application skills, but all AO2 skills (interpretation, analysis and evaluation) will also be rewarded. It is a different sort of question from a more straightforward one such as: **'Examine the problems some sociologists may face when using experiments in their research.' (20 marks) (AQA Jan 2009)**

You would score highly on this type of question provided you had revised the method and you could apply practical, ethical and theoretical (PET) factors systematically. However, you need to think about the Methods in Context question in a very different way. It is more difficult to prepare for because you will not know the specific issue or which methods will be available. You will have to think on your feet.

This is what you will need to focus on:

- the **specific issue or aspect** within education
- the **method you have chosen** — its strengths and limitations as they apply to this specific aspect/issue
- the **characteristics** of certain groups of people within the education system

**Application skills** are key to this type of question. Your task is to examine which features of your chosen method will bring out the best data from the specific issue, and which features may be a barrier to understanding the issue.

The **issue** from the sociology of education may be quite narrow. Examples have included: material deprivation and underachievement; anti-school subcultures; role of parents; girls' achievement or boys' underachievement.

**Examiner tip**

Although we have not included an item here, this question will always have one and there will be several hints on the strengths and weaknesses of the specific methods within it.

Let's take an example: **'Using material from Item A, assess the usefulness of either questionnaires or unstructured interviews for the study of pupil subcultures.'** We will look at unstructured interviews here.

## Dos and Don'ts

### Level 0 (L0)

Avoid writing at length about the particular issue making no reference to the method. You may have a great deal of knowledge of studies that might have been undertaken on the particular issue, but this is not the place to show it. If *all* you do in your answer is to examine the issue, you will score very poorly. If you do this you will achieve **Level 0** and will only score up to 6 or 7 marks out of 20.

### Level 1 (L1)

Avoid focusing just on the method itself, with little or no reference to the issue — pupil subcultures. If you write a sound account of the method, its strengths and limitations, appropriate concepts and the links to its methodological/theoretical base, you will achieve at Level 1 and will score up to 11 marks out of 20.

### Level 2 (L2)

If you demonstrate a good understanding of the method, but only apply it to education in general, you will achieve Level 2. You might refer to pupil subcultures and possibly how they are created, even add some material from a particular study, but the links to the usefulness of the given method would be weak. You will score up to 14 marks out of 20 for this type of response.

### Level 3 (L3)

This is what you should aim for. Think PET and apply the specific method to the issue, group and research setting in the question. So, if we take **pupil subcultures,** you should think about the following:

Research settings:

- Permission to be given (e.g. head, teachers, pupils, parents?) How to obtain it? (P)
- Where will the interviews take place — inside/outside school; at home; elsewhere?

Characteristics of those involved (e.g. students, teachers, researcher, parents, head teachers etc.):

- Anti-school groups. What kind of students? Not homogeneous: gender, ethnicity, social class. Accessibility of the group to the researcher? How visible are these groups? Unlikely to cooperate; difficult to access; possibly truants. How to gain trust and rapport? Can we get a sample? (P)
- Why might unstructured interviews work? What strengths and limitations would they have with this group of subjects? Theory? (T)
- The nature of the data = validity, reliability, representativeness (T)
- Interviewer effect? Possibility of group interviews? (P)
- Will the researcher need to lie to gain trust? What issues might the researcher face in pupil disclosure? Whose side are you on? (E)
- Will the groups benefit from taking part in the research? (E)

You *do not need* to include reference to studies, as there may not be a particular one that fits here. You just need to think about the given method and what its strengths and limitations would be in researching the specific issue and the settings where the research takes place and the characteristics of the people involved. You would score between 15 and 20 marks at **Level 3**.

## Paper 1 **Education**

> Read Item A below and answer questions 01 to 04 that follow.

### Item A

Sociologists of education have competing theories relating to the role that the education system plays in wider society. Some structural theorists look at education as responding to the needs of the society. This may be in terms of the functions it performs to maintain and perpetuate society, or its role in reproducing social inequality. Some sociologists see education as part of a meritocratic society, whereas others argue that processes within schools such as the hidden curriculum maintain an unequal society.

**(01) Explain what is meant by the term 'hidden curriculum'.** (2 marks)

e Briefly indicate that it includes areas not covered by the official subject curriculum.)

**(02) Suggest three policies that government or educational bodies have introduced to overcome what is seen as some pupils' cultural deprivation.** (6 marks)

e Write about policies that compensate for cultural (not material) deprivation, e.g. Sure Start).

**(03) Outline some of the reasons for the existence of anti-school subcultures.** (12 marks)

e Look for reasons such as streaming/teacher stereotyping, but do not describe studies.

**(04) Using material from Item A and elsewhere, assess the view that the modern education system is a meritocracy.** (20 marks)

e Evaluate the functionalist perspective and use other theoretical positions to criticise it.

### C-grade student

**(01)** Things like obedience to authority that schools teach pupils.

e **1/2 marks awarded.** The student has given an example rather than a definition of the term.

**(02)** Sending parents to classes so that they can help their children to read.

e **2/6 marks awarded.** The student has given only one possible policy here, but it is correct.

> **Examiner tip**
> Always check carefully that you have followed the instructions in the question.

**(03)** Willis studied one anti-school subculture. They were called the 'lads'. They were not interested in school but wanted to have a 'laff'. They spent their time messing around in school and wasting teachers' time. What they valued was manual work. The other groups were called the 'ear'oles' because they listened to the teachers and wanted to get qualifications. Willis said that education was really just preparation for working-class jobs and the lads were getting used to being bored at work.

Hargreaves went into school as a teacher and watched how the boys behaved in class. He found that many boys in the lower stream messed about and did not do well in school. The teachers did not expect them to do well and this caused an anti-school subculture.

**Examiner tip**
Remember the importance of reading the question carefully and then doing what it asks you to do.

ⓔ **6/12 marks awarded.** The student has shown some reasonable knowledge and understanding. Two reasons are given for the existence of anti-school subcultures but the knowledge is not well developed.

**(04)** Marxists and functionalists see the education system in different ways. Functionalists like Parsons and Durkheim see education as a meritocracy. This means that everyone has the same chance of doing well in school. Everyone has the opportunity to sit the same exams and the most talented will do best. Education teaches the next generation the skills necessary for work. Functionalists believe that society must be kept stable and in balance and that education is important in helping society to achieve social order. They say that people must have shared norms and values in order for society to work.

ⓔ This is a reasonable opening paragraph. There are links made between functionalism and ideas of meritocracy, but the student does not demonstrate the ways in which education can make this happen.

But Marxists disagree. They see education as a tool of the bourgeoisie to keep the working classes down. In school, children learn to be obedient and respect teachers. The system isn't fair for working-class children because they fail and as one sociologist said school teaches working-class boys how to get working-class jobs. The lads in his study did not try to succeed in school and formed their own anti-school subculture.

Bowles and Gintis said that the school system corresponded to capitalism and pupils are exploited by teachers. Capitalism needs workers who have been brainwashed to accept the power of the bourgeoisie. This happens through the hidden curriculum.

ⓔ Again the student shows some reasonable knowledge and understanding of theory. Evaluation is presented by juxtaposing Marxism and functionalism, but there is very little analysis here.

In conclusion, functionalists and Marxists disagree about the role of education. Marxists say that the idea of meritocracy is a myth because private schools exist for the rich. Most sociologists today reject the idea that education is fair for everyone because many working-class and some minority ethnic children and boys tend to underachieve in school.

🄔 12/20 marks awarded. **Overall, the answer demonstrates some relevant material that needs to be developed further to gain higher marks. The student fails to make any explicit reference to the material in Item A. The student would score more highly if he/she made reference to a 'modern education system'.**

### A-grade student

(01) This refers to things outside the official curriculum that pupils are taught, like punctuality, discipline, obedience to authority, values and beliefs; it can even mean sexism and racism.

🄔 2/2 marks awarded. This is a competent definition which includes several appropriate examples.

(02) There are many policies that do this. They include:

- Operation Headstart in the USA
- Sure Start in Britain
- Saturday schools
- Educational Action Zones

🄔 6/6 marks awarded. This student gives more responses than are asked for, but they are all correct. Even if one of the responses were incorrect, the student would still score full marks for the three correct ones.

(03) Sociologists have identified several reasons for the existence of anti-school subcultures. These are the effects of setting and streaming, labelling, laddism and resistance.

Hargreaves carried out the earliest work into anti-school subcultures. He showed that labelling boys and placing them in lower streams created anti-school feelings. Not only did the boys feel that they didn't count in school but their teachers treated them differently from the top stream. More recently, one of Peter Woods' pupil adaptations was rebellion where pupils rejected the means and goals of educational success and formed subcultures.

This reflects the behaviour of Willis' lads in *Learning to Labour*. Their anti-school subculture was mainly about having a 'laff'. They experienced school as alienating and as a result created an anti-school subculture as a coping strategy. Although he argued that these working-class lads were able to see through the system, it still operated to reproduce the class system.

Gillborn's work showed that teachers' racist attitudes towards black boys as 'troublemakers' led to anti-school resistance and challenge from these boys.

(e) **12/12 marks awarded.** The student shows good knowledge and understanding that is well focused on the question. He/she has been successful in interpreting, applying, analysing and evaluating the material.

**(04)** A meritocracy means a fair system where pupils will achieve success on the basis of their own efforts and ability. This functionalist view sees education as a system where the most talented and hard working will succeed.

(e) This is a good, clear introduction. The student demonstrates good knowledge and understanding of the concept.

According to Item A, structural theorists have competing views as to whether education is meritocratic. The view held by functionalists is that the education system performs an essential role in the selection process of people into appropriate roles in the economy. Parsons and Davis and Moore all saw education as meritocratic. They argue that individuals are not born intellectually equal. Intelligence is mainly genetic and the role of the education system is to select the most able for the most functionally important roles in society. Therefore, doctors and lawyers are naturally more intelligent than cleaners and porters. In Parsons' view a meritocratic education system is essential in a modern society. He saw the education system as a bridge between home and work. In the family, individuals are judged on 'particularistic' values; however, the education system, like the world of work, is based on 'universalistic' values.

(e) This paragraph develops the concept of meritocracy from the functionalist perspective. The student demonstrates an effective use of relevant examples and understands the relationship between home, school and work. There is a useful reference to Item A.

However, not all functionalists shared this view. Melvin Tumin said that Davis and Moore's work was too simplistic because there was no way of measuring the functional importance of particular jobs.

(e) This short paragraph includes an in-house criticism of functionalism.

On the other hand, structural theorists like Marxists see education as 'reproducing social inequality' (Item A) and completely reject the view that education is a meritocracy. They see that education really functions in the interest of the ruling class. Althusser saw education as an Ideological State Apparatus, which legitimates class inequality in society. Bowles and Gintis showed that there was a correspondence between the education system and the economy. The economy 'cast a long shadow over education'. This means that schools exert ideological control and are moulded according to the needs of capitalism. Through the hidden curriculum children learn to be obedient and to respect authority. Relationships between teachers and students are said to mirror those of employers and employees.

ⓔ This paragraph demonstrates sophisticated knowledge. The paragraph is both evaluative and analytical. The student is challenging the functionalist viewpoint by using the Marxist critique effectively. Good use is made of Item A again.

> Willis did an ethnographic study on 12 working-class boys where he showed that the boys could see through the system even though it meant that they still ended up with working-class jobs. He argued that rather than being meritocratic, the education system prepared working-class kids for working-class jobs.
>
> A recent report by the Rowntree Trust showed that far from there being greater equality in society, children — especially boys — from poorer backgrounds, were doing even worse than before. This clearly shows that the functionalists were wrong in their views. Recent evidence also shows that increasing numbers of successful professionals like lawyers, MPs, judges etc. generally come from Oxbridge and top public schools.
>
> With the introduction of parentocracy into education, middle-class parents are buying educational advantage for their children by moving to areas where neighbourhood schools are highly successful.

ⓔ These paragraphs make very good use of the item to show that a pupil's background has an important part to play in success, thus challenging the view that the modern education system is a meritocracy.

> In conclusion we can see that the system is a long way from being meritocratic and still today the wealthier your background, the more likely you are to succeed.

ⓔ 20/20 marks awarded. **Overall this student has demonstrated excellent sociological knowledge and understanding and has a sophisticated grasp of criticisms. The essay is sophisticated and coherent.**

# Methods in context

This question requires you to apply your knowledge and understanding
of sociological research methods to the study of this particular issue in
education.

**Read Item B and answer the question that follows.**

## Item B

### Investigating girls' increased educational achievement

From the 1970s feminist researchers in education have shown us that boys seeking
the attention of their teachers dominated classrooms. It wasn't that teachers were
consciously ignoring the girls, rather the space was more often taken over by the
boys. It is interesting to note that this did not prevent the progress of the girls. Other
factors were affecting their aspirations and achievements, for example subject
channelling, careers advice and parental expectations.

Some investigations into educational achievement use official statistics. These allow
researchers to look at trends and draw comparisons between the achievement of
girls and boys over time. They usually compare examination results at GCSE and
A-level and cover the whole school population. However, some researchers argue
that they lack validity.

Other researchers are more interested in the reasons why girls have moved ahead of
boys and why they continue to stay ahead. They tend to use unstructured interviews
in order to explore girls' attitudes and feelings about school, but access to schools is
often difficult. Girls' success may be affected by their teachers and peer groups.

**(05) Using material from Item B and elsewhere, assess the strengths and limitations of one
of the following methods for the study of girls' increased educational achievement:**
   **(i)  official statistics**
   **(ii) unstructured interviews**
                                                                                    (20 marks)

ⓔ Before you choose your method read the section on Methods in Context on pages 46–47.

## C-grade student

**(05) (ii)** Unstructured interviews

Item B says that 'other researchers are more interested in the reasons why girls have moved ahead of boys and why they continue to stay ahead. They tend to use unstructured interviews to explore girls' attitudes and feelings about school'. Feminists like Dale Spender say that the classroom is male dominated. Her methods have been criticised because she was teaching and researching in the classroom at the same time, but this is really impossible to do.

**ⓔ** The student lifts a sentence from Item B, but does not expand on it. The reference to Spender does not explain her methodology so does not develop the argument. The student could have explained how the interviews were conducted in more detail. This paragraph is a Level 0 response because it refers to the issue only.

Interactionists like unstructured interviews because they can get rapport and *verstehen*. The girls might also be more open if the interview isn't formal like structured interviews. The researcher could interview girls in top sets and ask them about their attitudes to school and careers. The researcher couldn't find this out from statistics. Stanworth did interviews with teachers in secondary schools, but she didn't actually speak to girls. She found that male teachers hardly knew the girls in their classes and assumed they would become secretaries.

**ⓔ** This paragraph includes some relevant Level 1 material about the chosen method, together with some stated theory and undeveloped concepts. The reference to the method and how the girls can discuss their feelings is a Level 2 point, but this needs further development to make it Level 3, perhaps being able to discuss the girls' aspirations and whether they work hard for their exams.

One problem the researcher may face is getting into the school to talk to the girls as sometimes heads don't like having researchers around. There's also a problem with taking up teaching time especially as unstructured interviews take a long time and they may be wasting class time.

**ⓔ** The student makes two Level 2 points about method here, but they are not linked specifically to the achievement of girls.

In conclusion, many sociologists use unstructured interviews as part of triangulation in their research. This makes for more validity and reliability. Positivists don't like it but interpretivists and feminists do because it is more valid.

**ⓔ** This could have been a better conclusion if the student had explained how triangulation enhanced validity and reliability. By linking the concepts we can only assume that the student does not know the differences between them. Theories are stated rather than being expanded.

**e** **13/20 marks awarded. Overall, the student gains Level 1 marks for method and theory and makes two reasonable Level 2 points and one weaker Level 2 point.**

**(05) (i)** Official statistics

Item B shows that researchers use official statistics (O/S) on educational achievement to see trends and to make comparisons over time. This would be very useful because it would allow the researcher to trace exactly when girls started to move ahead of the boys. Many commentators argue that the introduction of the National Curriculum and coursework at GCSE helped girls to move ahead of boys, and we might be able to pinpoint this to a particular date. However, as the gap has still not narrowed since coursework was withdrawn from many subjects, we might have to search the stats for other possible factors.

**e** This is a good start. The student refers to the item and makes a Level 3 point linking the method with girls' achievement. The last sentence is also evaluative.

A great advantage in using O/S is that the researcher would not have to get past any gatekeepers to get the data. Heads are usually resistant to researchers coming into their schools and where girls' achievements are outdoing boys, they may feel defensive that they aren't helping the boys enough and refuse to give their consent. Parents are also powerful gatekeepers and might also refuse to have their daughters interviewed by strangers, especially if they have not met the researchers themselves. This means then that O/S have more ethical credibility and are not produced by deception or lack of informed consent.

**e** There are two Level 2 points here on gatekeepers. The point about heads being resistant becomes a Level 3 point in relation to them becoming defensive that they are perhaps helping girls more than boys. The point about parents and daughters is also Level 2. Ethical issues are dealt with in a sophisticated manner.

O/S avoids these problems. Positivist researchers rate O/S highly as they see sociology like the natural sciences providing reliable, objective data that can be used to demonstrate trends and make comparisons over time. As every school's results are recorded, the data are both representative and generalisable. It is easy to make comparisons between regions and before and after educational policies possibly favouring girls, such as GIST, WISE were introduced. It may be useful to compare single-sex girls' schools with coeducational ones to see if girls do even better in schools which are single sex.

**e** There are good theoretical points made here with several appropriate concepts (Level 1 points). The reference to 'every school' is Level 2 as it is a characteristic of all schools, and the reference to GIST and WISE is Level 3, as it is specific to the issue.

However, one of the problems with O/S is that they are open to manipulation. Many governments have massaged figures especially with unemployment. This could be the case with league tables for 5+ GCSE A*–C. They don't tell us about the actual subjects taken, and some new academies were including courses like BTEC, which were claimed to be equivalent to five GCSEs. Also we cannot understand the motivation of the girls by looking at statistics and whether, or if, it is different from that of the boys.

**e** The student makes a Level 1 point criticising the possibility of manipulating statistics. The criticism is Level 2 as it relates to education statistics in general. The reference to 'motivation of the girls' needs developing to achieve a Level 3.

In conclusion, O/S can be used in a variety of ways to understand this topic. Perhaps the most useful way of gaining a thorough understanding would be to combine O/S data with some primary research. This would give us more valid insight because we would get closer to the reality of the situation and interpretivist methodology would allow us to get closer to how the girls themselves feel about their lives in school and their aspirations for the future.

**e** 20/20 marks awarded. **Overall this is a very sophisticated and conceptually strong response. The student has identified strengths and limitations of O/S and has successfully applied the method to the issue. There is evidence of all levels in this response: several sound Level 1 points on methodology and theory (PET); four points at Level 2; and two sophisticated points at Level 3. It would be difficult to do better under examination conditions.**

# Research methods

These questions permit you to draw examples from any areas of sociology with which you are familiar.

**(06)  Explain what is meant by the term 'validity'.**                              (2 marks)

ⓔ Many students confuse validity with reliability. Make sure that you know the difference.

**(07)  Suggest two reasons why some sociologists use snowball sampling.**            (4 marks)

ⓔ Don't waste time in explaining how it is done. Just give two reasons, e.g. no sampling frame available.

**(08)  Suggest two reasons why sociologists wish their samples to be representative.**   (4 marks)

ⓔ Positivists value this, so think about generalisability, trends and patterns.

**(09)  Examine the reasons why some sociologists prefer to use participant observation in their research.**                                         (20 marks)

ⓔ Think PET, different types of participant observation and reasons for their use. Appropriate concepts will score.

### C-grade student

**(06)**  This is whether the data are accurate.

ⓔ **0/2 marks awarded.** This is too vague to score any marks. 'Accuracy' is not a sufficient definition without more clarification.

**(07)**  You can't find enough people by yourself. Laurie Taylor used one.

ⓔ **1/4 marks awarded.** There is only one partially correct answer here. The reference to Laurie Taylor does not tell us why he used the technique.

**(08)**  So they can generalise their data to reveal information about the whole research population. They want their findings to be valid.

ⓔ **2/4 marks awarded.** The first response here is appropriate, but the second is incorrect.

**(09)** Some sociologists like interpretivists use participant observation (PO) in their research. They argue that it gives them meanings and motivations because the researcher joins in with the people being studied. It gives deeper insight and empathy. Positivists would not use PO. It doesn't give numerical data that would allow them to find patterns and make comparisons.

There are two types of participant observation, covert and overt. One reason you might use PO is because it is the only possible method to study the group. This is true of deviant groups who don't want to be studied by sociologists. Covert PO is a good method for this. James Patrick used covert participant observation in his study of a Glasgow gang because he wanted to find out what it was really like inside a gang. He couldn't have given the gang questionnaires to fill in because they would have refused and they were very aggressive.

**e** This is a sound introduction. The student correctly identifies the perspective associated with participant observation (PO) and develops it. These paragraphs give a limited positivist criticism and outline two main types of participant observation together with a basic description of the method. The student has also identified one reason why a researcher would choose to use PO.

Laud Humphreys also used covert participant observation in *Tearoom Trade*. He became a 'watch queen' for men having sex in public toilets. He did not take part, but he was covert, because they did not know that he was researching them. He had to write up notes in the car. What Humphreys did next was to take down the registration numbers of the men's cars. He then included these men in his health questionnaire to find out if they were married or not. Although it was unethical, he couldn't have found out his information any other way. If he had interviewed them, they might have lied.

Many sociologists would argue that covert PO would be the best method of observation because it avoids a lot of problems like the Hawthorne effect and gives the researcher more in-depth insight. However, it can put researchers into dangerous situations and they are forced to lie about themselves. This is why other researchers will use overt PO where they will explain who they are and why they are there.

**Examiner tip**

Try to avoid lengthy descriptions of research studies in your answers. In this case the question asks for the 'reasons' for the use of the method.

**e** This is a lengthy description of one study. The student gives some reasons for the use of covert PO, but there is some loss of focus as he/she gives disadvantages of the method.

**Examiner tip**

The student focuses more on an 'advantages versus disadvantages' approach to the question. It is important to answer the question that is written on the exam paper, rather than the one you might have prepared.

There is also overt participant observation but this gives the Hawthorne effect because people know that they are being studied and they act differently. This makes the data invalid, but it is more ethical than covert because it avoids deception and lack of informed consent.

In conclusion, positivists do not use participant observation because they see it as unreliable and unscientific. Interpretivists see participant observation as one of the best methods to understand social interaction and to really understand individuals' meanings and motivations.

**e** This is a brief but reasonable conclusion.

ⓔ **14/20 marks awarded. The student has focused on some of the reasons for the use of participant observation, but has lost some focus by including material on disadvantages. It is very important to be clear what the question is asking you to do. This response also has some useful evaluation.**

**A-grade student**

**(06)** Validity means if the data measure what the researcher set out to measure. It means whether the material collected is close to the true reality of the situation.

ⓔ **2/2 marks awarded.** This is a clear definition.

**(07)** There is no sampling frame and the samples are hard to access. They are often in deviant or secret groups.

ⓔ **4/4 marks awarded.** The student has produced three possible correct responses here. Any two will count.

**(08)** If the funding body is the government it wants to make sure that it can talk about the wider population.

By having a representative sample sociologists are aiming to avoid distortion/ bias because the sample is a good cross-section of the target population.

So they don't have an atypical sample.

ⓔ **4/4 marks awarded.** The student has produced more than two appropriate reasons and would score full marks for any two.

**(09)** Participant observation is a qualitative method used by interpretivists. It allows the researcher to study a group in order to gain in-depth understanding of what it is like to be a member of such a group. It can be either overt where the group being studied are aware of the researcher's presence and aims; or covert where the researcher's identity is hidden from the group. One reason why covert participant observation is a very popular method for studying deviant and secret groups is that it allows the observer to get inside the group without the members knowing that they are being researched. It produces the most valid data as it is as close as a researcher can get to the meanings of social action and the reasons why such action takes place.

ⓔ This is a very clear and coherent introduction. The student has put the method into a theoretical context and has started to look at reasons for its use.

Interpretivists choose covert participant observation because it gives them access to groups not otherwise available, especially groups who would not respond to questionnaires or structured interviews. For example, both Patrick and Humphreys used covert participant observation to study hard-to-access groups. It helped them to see from the inside what the lives of these people were really like.

ⓔ This is a well-focused paragraph. It identifies two reasons and uses supporting evidence in a concise and relevant manner. The student avoids the pitfall of lengthy descriptions.

> Goffman also found that being covert in a US mental hospital enabled him to see processes at work that even the staff weren't aware of, such as 'making out'.
>
> Another important reason for using covert participant observation was shown by William Foote Whyte. He used an informer (a gatekeeper) to gain access to his research group. Although there were problems with his research, he showed the importance of standing back and listening. He said 'I learned answers to questions I hadn't thought of asking'. He wouldn't have gained the same kind of information if he had used questionnaires or structured interviews.

ⓔ This is another well-focused paragraph that identifies another appropriate reason for participant observation.

> However, there are many reasons why researchers would choose overt over covert participant observation. If the researcher is being truthful with the group members, they are more likely to gain their trust and build a rapport with them. This will produce more in-depth, valid data and the researcher will gain greater insight into their actions. It solves the problem of deception and prevents any possible danger of illegality, as the researcher would not feel pressured into getting too involved. However, it produces the Hawthorne effect and this might challenge the validity of the data. On the other hand the researcher can record events openly rather than having to rely on their memory. Sometimes, covert participant observation is the only method that allows a researcher to gain valuable insight, such as Fielding in his study of a right-wing political group, even when the BSA sees it as unethical and to be avoided.
>
> Eileen Barker justified her reasons for doing overt research into the Moonies by saying that she did not want to deceive the members. Although they were wary of her at first, she soon became a trusted stranger and many of them confided in her.
>
> In conclusion, there are many reasons why interpretivists see that this method is very useful in gaining valid data from within the group being studied that could not be found by another method. However, positivists would criticise it as unreliable and unrepresentative.

ⓔ 20/20 marks awarded. **The essay demonstrates a range of reasons for the use of participant observation in research. It is conceptually detailed and well focused on reasons. There is some slight imbalance as most of the studies are covert and less is made of the overt dimension. There is a brief but reasoned conclusion.**

# Paper 2 **Education**

**Read Item A below and answer questions 01 to 04 that follow.**

## Item A

Some of the main causes of the underachievement of some ethnic minority students relate to factors within the school. Negative labelling and stereotypical assumptions by teachers can often result in some ethnic minority students acting up to their label. There is some evidence to show that the gap between success and failure between some ethnic groups is widening rather than narrowing. However social class and gender are also very significant factors that cut across ethnicity. Indeed some schools may be seen to operate a gender regime.

**(01) Explain what is meant by the term 'gender regime'.**                                        (2 marks)

ⓔ 'Regime' is a type of system often linked to control, so think how a gender 'system' would operate within education.

**(02) Suggest three aspects of the hidden curriculum.**                                           (6 marks)

ⓔ Give three examples here such as learning obedience to authority.

**(03) Outline some of the reasons why females now achieve higher results than males in the education system.**                                                                       (12 marks)

ⓔ Your focus here must be on girls. Reasons may be from in-school and outside factors.

**(04) Using material from Item A and elsewhere, assess sociological explanations of the differential educational achievement of ethnic groups.**                                 (20 marks)

ⓔ Don't fall into the trap of assuming ethnic groups are homogeneous. The question doesn't say 'minority ethnic' so look at 'majority' ethnic too. Some groups such as Chinese students are achieving very highly, while white working-class boys are not. Class and gender cut across ethnicity.

**C-grade student**

**(01)** This is where girls and boys are separated into different subjects like girls into netball and boys into football.

ⓔ **1/2 marks awarded.** This is a relatively simplistic definition, but the student has some limited awareness of gender selection and gains 1 mark for a partial explanation.

**(02)** The hidden curriculum is a Marxist term that shows that schools are part of the capitalist system. It is all those things that are not taught officially and you can't really explain how it happens, but pupils learn to obey teachers.

ⓔ **2/6 marks awarded.** The student has shown some understanding of the term, but has not provided three different aspects. 'Pupils learn to obey teachers' gains 2 marks.

**(03)** Since the introduction of the National Curriculum, girls have become much more successful than boys at GCSE. Since 1990 there has been a 10% gap between the results of boys and girls. Here are some of the reasons why girls are more successful.

The introduction of coursework since the 1980s has helped girls achieve higher grades, as they tend to work more consistently than boys over the year and so get better marks for their coursework projects.

The changing position of women in society (economic independence and lone-parent mothers) has shown girls the importance of having a career. So they have become more career-minded now than in the 1970s. Sue Sharpe showed that girls' priorities in the 1970s and the 1990s were different. Although she found that in the 1970s girls mainly wanted to get married and have a family, in the 1990s girls wanted a career first.

The National Curriculum means that boys and girls have to study core subjects like science and maths and so girls have not been able to drop science, and have shown that they can achieve as well or sometimes even better than the boys.

Parents' attitudes have also changed. They now encourage their daughters to do well in school, so we can see that all these things work together to put girls ahead of boys.

ⓔ **9/12 marks awarded.** The student gives several reasons for the achievement of girls. There is sound knowledge and understanding and interpretation is well focused. There is some explicit evaluation.

**(04)** There are several reasons that sociologists put forward to explain the underachievement of ethnic minority groups. First, schools and teachers have been accused of being institutionally racist.

ⓔ Many students assume that pupils from all ethnic minorities underachieve. Is this student going to do this?

Bernard Coard said that the British education system made the black child 'educationally subnormal'. Teachers treat black boys as troublemakers and often see them as aggressive and as a threat in the classroom. Jayleigh School is an example of a school that was racist. In the school, streaming was closely linked to race. Asian students were placed in lower streams and so they were not entered for as many GCSEs as white students.

(e) Here the student has differentiated between two groups of students, if only implicitly, by examining the positions of black boys and Asian pupils.

> According to Cecile Wright, ethnic minority pupils in primary school were treated differently from white pupils. Asian pupils were ignored by teachers who thought that they could not speak English. Black boys were treated unfairly. They were expected to behave badly and were punished by the teacher. Black pupils are much more likely to be permanently excluded from school compared with white pupils. This is due to the racism of many teachers. Other sociologists have seen language and home background as important factors and some parents have set up black-only schools.

(e) **12/20 marks awarded.** There is reasonable knowledge and understanding here. However, there is a lack of balanced argument in the response as the student assumes that there are only differences in underachievement. There is no reference made to those ethnic groups that are doing very well in education, such as Chinese and African students. There is no reference made to Item A and the essay lacks a conclusion.

## A-grade student

**(01)** This is difficult to describe. It's a school run on gender lines. Usually patriarchy dominates, the hierarchy is male and there are sexist attitudes in the school that aren't challenged by staff.

(e) **2/2 marks awarded.** This is a good attempt at a difficult concept. The student has a notion of a ruling system and one that favours one gender over the other.

**(02)** The hidden curriculum includes a range of aspects. There is fragmentation of knowledge where the curriculum is split into different subjects and times of day, so pupils don't have any power over timing and what they learn.

Pupils have to be punctual and learn to be disciplined. It also includes gender socialisation and even how to learn to accept boredom.

(e) **6/6 marks awarded.** This response includes at least six different and relevant aspects. However, it is important not to get carried away and write very full responses to this question, as timing is important. The student gains 2 marks for each of three correct aspects.

**(03)** Since the 1990s there has been a consistent gap between the achievement of boys and girls. Girls now outperform boys by at least 10% at GCSE and the gap has closed at A-level too. One reason identified for girls' success has been changing parental attitudes. Parents are now placing more emphasis on their daughters' education. They have higher expectations of their daughters than of their sons.

There is evidence that in the past girls did not actually underachieve, but the dice were loaded against them. Under the tripartite system, girls generally achieved higher 11+ scores than boys but allocation to grammar schools was unfair. This may be an indication that girls have not suddenly outperformed boys in education, but that overall factors in wider society, including sexist attitudes towards women, had not given them equal opportunities.

Sue Sharpe claimed that girls in the 1970s placed little emphasis on educational success. However, two decades later she found that girls had changed their attitudes to educational achievement and wanted a career first.

New policies in education (e.g. GIST and WISE) and the National Curriculum resulted in a greater achievement of girls. Girls now study what were traditionally seen as 'male' areas and they have been very successful. There are many other reasons for girls' achievement. Feminists would argue that raised awareness of women's social position and wider social changes in the family, such as the availability and use of contraceptives such as the pill, more female breadwinners in families and more women employed in professional and managerial roles in the labour market have been very significant in providing role models for girls.

**Examiner tip**

In a question on reasons for girls' achievement, try to avoid giving reasons why boys are not doing as well.

ⓔ **12/12 marks awarded.** This student has shown sound and conceptually informed knowledge and understanding and has been successful in interpreting, applying, analysing and evaluating material relevant to the question.

**(04)** It is important to say that ethnic minority groups do not all perform the same in education. In fact, the highest achieving groups include groups such as Chinese, Indian and some African students, whereas in the lowest achieving groups there are Afro-Caribbean, Bangladeshi and Turkish students. An interesting fact is that those at the bottom of the achievement ladder are white working-class boys who form a majority ethnic group.

ⓔ This is an impressive start. The student is aware that 'ethnic minority' groups do not constitute a homogeneous category and has included some examples of differential educational achievement to illustrate this.

Many early sociological explanations focused on cultural and language factors as the causes of underachievement. More recently, however, the focus has widened to include what happens in school as well as racism more generally.

ⓔ This student clearly understands that this is a complex question and demonstrates that explanations have changed over time. Evaluation is explicit here.

In the past, language barriers were identified as a major cause of underachievement for students where English was not the main language spoken at home. However, Ballard and Driver's research showed that language difficulties were no longer an issue by the time the student reached 16. These students of this age were as fluent in English as their classmates. Today most sociologists would reject language factors as the major cause of underachievement.

ⓔ In this paragraph, the student both identifies and analyses the issue of language effectively. It is evaluative and the student makes reference to appropriate research.

Cultural deprivation was also blamed for the underachievement of some groups. For example, in his study Ken Pryce suggested that Afro-Caribbean families were 'turbulent'. He argued that these families did not provide adequate cultural capital for their children. Some New Right sociologists and politicians saw the higher proportion of lone-parent families within this group as yet another reason for their failure.

(e) Both of these paragraphs provide material relevant to the argument that underachievement in education is related to home factors. This should now be balanced by evidence of in-school factors.

However, the Swann Report challenged many of these stereotypical views and said that if social class wasn't a factor, these students would not be disadvantaged. The report claimed that lower social class position accounted for at least 80% of educational underachievement. Social class was more significant for some groups, such as those from Bangladesh and Pakistan and some Afro-Caribbean students, as these groups are mainly working class. Therefore issues such as material deprivation may also play a significant role.

(e) This is good analysis and evaluation of the findings of the Swann Report.

Other arguments blamed the education system itself. Bernard Coard's research is particularly significant in examining disadvantage. He showed that black pupils were made to feel 'educationally subnormal', for example, the association of 'white' with 'good' and 'black' with 'bad' in children's literature. In 1999, Ofsted identified the British education system as institutionally racist in terms of its curriculum and personnel.

The Jayleigh study showed that in inner-city schools, ethnic minority pupils were at a disadvantage in terms of GCSE entries, being in lower sets and having to achieve higher grades in order to be seen as successful. Wright's study found that some ethnic minority groups received less attention from staff. Teachers' perceptions were seen as stereotypical; although Asian students were seen as 'good', black students were seen as disruptive and disobedient.

(e) The student now takes up the alternative, critical positions, looking at factors pointing to institutional racism.

In conclusion, it is clear that this is a complex issue. Some of the highest achieving groups are from ethnic minorities. We also need to take into account that we cannot separate ethnicity from social class and gender. Research on interaction between staff and students, including studies such as Fuller's and Mac an Ghaill's on some minority ethnic students, has shown that pupils can resist negative labels and teacher expectations and still be successful in the education system.

(e) **20/20 marks awarded. This is a very sophisticated response that demonstrates high-level knowledge and understanding of arguments and evidence and the essential skills of evaluation and analysis. The student has shown a clear rationale in organising the material leading to a distinct conclusion.**

# Methods in context

This question requires you to apply your knowledge and understanding of sociological research methods to the study of this particular issue in education.

Read Item B and answer the question that follows.

## Item B

### Investigating the role of parents in their children's educational achievement

Many sociologists would agree that parents have a significant impact on their children's educational success or failure. Parents are characterised by many differences, especially in terms of social class and their own educational experiences, for example whether they have a university education. This is likely to affect how they interact with heads and teachers. With greater cultural and material capital, many middle-class parents are able to pay for private tutors to help their children with revision for examinations or to pay for selective schooling.

Interactionists prefer unstructured interviews as they help to make respondents feel at ease and so they provide rich, in-depth data even on sensitive topics. However, they are time consuming and schools may not want their teaching disrupted.

Postal questionnaires can cover a much wider area and a greater number of respondents. To save postage, pupils could be given them to take home and return them when completed. However, parents may choose not to respond unless it is clear what benefit there is for them or their children.

(05) Using material from Item B and elsewhere, assess the strengths and limitations of one of the following methods for investigating the role of parents in their children's educational achievement:
  (i)  unstructured interviews
  (ii) postal questionnaires                                    (20 marks)

ⓔ The item refers to social class and the cultural and material capital of parents. These are useful pointers to link to the suitability of your chosen method.

### C-grade student

(05) (ii) Questionnaires are used for social surveys. They usually have a set of closed questions. These produce quantitative data which are preferred by positivists. Postal questionnaires are either sent by post or put on the internet. If a researcher wants to study parents' role in their children's achievement, questionnaires would be a quick way to get information.

> Many working-class parents have jobs with long hours, sometimes shifts, so they couldn't really be interviewed easily or go into the school to talk to a researcher. Questionnaires are filled in at home and this is a practical advantage as parents can take time to think about their answers.

**e** The student makes some Level 1 points, including reference to theory here. There is also a Level 2 point on working-class parents and inconvenience.

> Pupils could be given them to take home and this would save on postage, so makes them even cheaper than interviews. A disadvantage of this would be that they could get lost or forgotten by pupils and pass the date to return them. There could easily be a low response rate and only interested parents like middle-class ones would return them. This lowers representativeness.

**e** This paragraph contains Level 1 points on practical issues and two Level 2 points on: the characteristics of pupils — losing or forgetting the forms; and middle-class parents — being more likely to return the forms.

> Postal questionnaires don't have many open-ended questions, because people don't like spending time filling in long answers. So they would not be in-depth and interpretivists wouldn't choose them as they would be mainly quantitative.

**e** Here the student makes Level 1 points on the method, along with some evaluation on theory.

> There may be problems with some parents not understanding the language. They may be new to the country and their English may be poor, or they may have poor literacy anyway. They could misunderstand the questions and there would be no-one to explain what they mean. This would lower validity, but there's greater reliability as there would be a wide range of parents' responses and different cultural practices and views could be seen.

**e** This paragraph has Level 2 points on the characteristics of some parents — language difficulties as a result of being new to the country, poor literacy, and different cultural practices. However, this last point needs more development.

> However, as the item says, they have a wide coverage and can reach lots of respondents. They have practical advantages like saving time and cost and you don't have to get permission to send them out or interview people. On the other hand, parents may not want to answer questions on how they bring up their children, as it's a personal thing.

**e** This paragraph partly repeats earlier points made plus provides some additional material on the issue being personal, but this is not developed. The point about not needing permission to send the questionnaires out from schools is incorrect.

ⓔ **14/20 marks awarded. Overall there are several sound Level 1 points including some reference to theory and three, potentially four, Level 2 points.**

**A-grade student**

**(05) (ii)** Many researchers use questionnaires in their research and postal questionnaires are especially popular because they save money (not paying people to hand them out and then collect them again). Usually they have closed, pre-coded questions, but it is possible to include some open-ended questions for respondents to elaborate on their answers if they choose. Positivists would support the use of questionnaires as they collect highly representative, reliable data that can be generalised. They want to find the laws of social behaviour and this method can show patterns, trends and correlations that can be compared between groups and over time. Postal questionnaires have a greater risk of a low response rate than those that are handed out, but because they can be mailed, they can have a wider coverage and contact a greater number of respondents (Item B).

ⓔ This is an excellent introduction which gives several characteristics and practical advantages of the method. The student locates it methodologically, makes reference to the item and produces a disadvantage, which is dealt with evaluatively. These are all Level 1 points.

Practical advantages are savings on time and cost. There's little expense in sending them out and as the item says, pupils can take them home. There is a problem with this delivery system as some pupils may not actually deliver them if they think they are about their behaviour, or they may simply forget to hand them to parents

ⓔ Here the student makes a Level 1 point on time and cost and a Level 2 point on the disadvantages of giving them to pupils to deliver.

Another practical factor is there is no problem accessing parents. Questionnaires are just posted home. However, if the researcher wanted to get teachers' views of parental roles, that may be different. They would have to get permission from the head teacher to send in the questionnaires to the schools and then teachers, who are very busy, may not want to complete them. Parental role is a sensitive issue and teachers may feel it is not for them to comment on how any parent behaves in relation to parents' evenings or whether they come in to talk of their child's progress. This is usually a matter between teachers and parents themselves and there might have to be another level of consent from parents to allow teachers to do this. All of this serves to make access a real problem.

ⓔ Accessibility is initially dealt with as a Level 1 issue, but developed into a Level 2 (teachers are very busy) and further extended into Level 3 point in reference to teachers and their position in relation to parents.

Ethical issues can also affect the responses to postal questionnaires. Both privacy and confidentiality can pose problems for the researcher. When parents are filling in the forms, they could feel exposed and embarrassed if the questions assume a certain level of interest they should have in their child's schooling. Working-class parents, in particular may feel that they are again being judged on not being 'good enough' parents (especially at a time when they are criticised by the media for not watching what their children are eating). Also, as Douglas found, just because a parent doesn't turn up at parents' evenings and open evenings doesn't mean that they don't care about their child's progress, but perhaps they have work or childcare commitments.

**e** This paragraph demonstrates extended Level 3 thinking on ethical issues. There is sophisticated knowledge and understanding of the position of working-class parents feeling that they are being 'judged again'. The reference to Douglas is evaluative.

Middle-class parents who have more cultural capital are more at ease with teachers, they are often highly educated professionals themselves and speak the 'same language' as educationalists. They would see it as part of their parental duty to complete these questionnaires if it makes them seem good parents and could be of benefit to their child's schooling.

**e** Here the student makes another Level 2 point about middle-class parents that goes further and develops the usefulness of possessing cultural capital into a Level 3 point.

In conclusion, the postal questionnaire as we have shown is not the best method for this type of research. The researcher would gain more valid and in-depth data by using unstructured interviews. However, they would still find that middle-class parents would be more comfortable discussing the educational experience and achievement of their children, because of their cultural capital. This might lead the researchers to assume there are class differences in parental roles when in fact these may be the result of differences in language codes.

**e** **20/20 marks awarded. This is a reasoned, justified conclusion. It is interesting that the student makes reference to the other given method as being more advantageous, but produces a sophisticated reason (at Level 3) why it would also pose problems for the outcome of the research. It would be difficult for any student to produce a better response than this in an examination situation. The student demonstrates very sound knowledge and understanding of the method and its theoretical location. There are at least four Level 2 points and three Level 3 points, two of which are extended and evaluated.**

# Research methods

> These questions permit you to draw examples from any areas of sociology with which you are familiar.

**(06) Explain what is meant by the term 'sampling frame'.** (2 marks)

ⓔ Make sure that you explain the term. You must have the notion of 'list' to score fully.

**(07) Suggest two ethical issues associated with the use of covert observation.** (4 marks)

ⓔ Make sure that you are giving 'ethical' reasons. Remember that danger to the observer is not an ethical but a practical issue.

**(08) Suggest two reasons why sociologists find official statistics useful.** (4 marks)

ⓔ Again care is needed. Some students misread questions and might see this as asking for problems of official statistics (O/S), therby losing a possible 4 marks.

**(09) Examine some of the factors that influence a researcher's choice of method.** (20 marks)

ⓔ This is a popular question and one that you should be well prepared for. Think PET and relevant concepts. You need to be analytical and evaluative in your answer.

**C-grade student**

**(06)** This is like the electoral register.

ⓔ **1/2 marks awarded.** The student has given an example rather than a definition, but it is a correct example and scores 1 mark.

**(07)** Because the people know they are being observed the Hawthorne effect happens.
The researcher may be putting him/herself in danger.
Deception.

ⓔ **2/4 marks awarded.** The student's first issue is incorrect, as 'covert' is confused with 'overt'. The second issue is a practical one not an ethical one and only the third is correct.

**(08)** Time and money.
Because there is a large dark figure.

ⓔ **0/4 marks awarded.** The student does not gain any marks here. Time and money could be made relevant by qualifying them, as in 'saves time and money'. It is not clear what is meant by the second reason.

(09) Many factors can influence a sociologist's choice of method. This can depend on what the researcher is investigating and using the most suitable method to do so. An example would be Durkheim in his famous work on suicide. Durkheim used official statistics available at the time.

e Although the student refers to 'many factors', there is little development of this point. The example is descriptive and does not explain why Durkheim used this method.

Sociologists choose methods based on what kind of sociologist they are. For example, a functionalist or feminist would probably use different methods. Functionalists are linked with positivism and feminists are linked with interpretivist methods. Functionalists look on society as a 'real' thing and want to get quantitative data like official statistics.

e Some of the points about theoretical preference are stated rather than explained and developed.

Interpretivists, on the other hand, look on society through the eyes of the people within that society. They prefer qualitative data because they are more in-depth and more valid. With secondary data they use content analysis and look for themes and meanings in diaries, letters and TV programmes.

e There is some reasonable development here and the student has developed some of the theoretical factors influencing choice of method.

Other practical factors that can affect choice are time and money. If they want to carry out a study over a long time and have enough funds, they would choose the longitudinal survey. This would let them see how society is changing over time. Just like the TV programme Seven Up where we could see how children from different backgrounds had different lives. This took place over many years and isn't very practical. With PO there are also practical issues of getting in, staying in and getting out. Sociologists who wish to look at one particular group may use a case study, which is good for accuracy.

e There are practical factors behind choice here. Although the programme is not a result of sociological research, it is widely used to show a longitudinal study, and is therefore justifiable, but the points are simply stated. The reference to use of a case study fails to explain why it is useful.

Ethical issues are another important factors that researchers have to take into account. Zimbardo's study of the prison shows how easy it is to harm people under study and he also went native in his role as prison governor. It is possible to use laboratory experiments but not very often as they are artificial. This is why the field experiment is used.

e **13/20 marks awarded. The student has understood that there are three types of factors — practical, ethical and theoretical — and attempts to look at each of**

these. In the final paragraph there is reference to ethical issues but this is limited in development. The essay comes to an abrupt end without a reasoned conclusion, thus losing some valuable points for evaluation.

**A-grade student**

**(06)** A sampling frame is a list of names or addresses of the target population that the researcher chooses the sample from. It can be a school register or a doctor's list of patients.

**e** **2/2 marks awarded.** This is a sound definition and includes appropriate examples as well.

**(07)** Lack of informed consent.
Researcher may have to take part in illegal activities.
Putting the lives of others at risk.

**e** **4/4 marks awarded.** There are three correct issues here and any two would score. It is useful in these short-answer questions to add a third possibility just in case one of the others is considered incorrect.

**(08)** Positivists argue that they are both valid and reliable.
Positivists believe that they are objective hard data.
They cover a wide population and so are representative.

**e** **4/4 marks awarded.** The student has produced several possible correct reasons here. Validity has been qualified by linking it to positivists.

**(09)** There are three main factors that influence a researcher's choice of method. These are practical, ethical and theoretical. Some researchers argue that the most important of these is theoretical, as the method chosen by the researcher will depend on how they think society should be studied.

**e** This is a sound introduction. The student has referred to the P, E and T factors and already made an evaluative point.

There are many practical factors that have to be taken into account, such as time, cost, access, opportunity and danger. Perhaps the most important is cost, because this affects a lot of things. If you have enough money you can have a large-scale survey research team, use many interviewers and other people to collate the data. With little money, you might have to work alone and use participant observation.

**e** The student is focused on the question, linking factors to choice of method. There is good application and analysis. It is important not to confuse methods with topic of research here.

Who funds the research is also very important. Government bodies may take ownership of the findings and not allow them to be published. Funding bodies may dictate the methods and this may go against the approach of the researcher. Project Camelot is an example of research that was funded by the Pentagon and the aims weren't known to the researchers. When they found out, many left the project.

(e) This is an important paragraph. Students often fail to refer to funding bodies and these may well be the key influence on choice of research methods. The student has also implicitly referred to ethical factors here.

Generally, functionalists use positivistic approaches, as they believe that social reality is capable of being observed and measured. This means that they use methods that produce quantitative, reliable data. They look for cause and effect relationships, so they compare social facts and investigate trends and patterns in social behaviour. For secondary data they prefer official statistics, like Durkheim's use of suicide statistics in different European countries in the nineteenth century. They see reliability and representativeness as very important, because they want to generalise and make predictions.

However, interpretivists follow Weber, who argued that sociologists should look for meanings of social action and use *verstehen* in their work. They prefer qualitative methods — like unstructured interviews and participant observation, where the researcher can become one of the group and see interactions taking place. They want validity in the research.

(e) These two paragraphs focus on the theoretical context of methods. Sound links are made between sociological perspective and choice of method. The student also uses relevant concepts appropriately.

Laud Humphreys in *Tearoom Trade* used covert participant observation when he took the role of 'watch queen'. He was able to look at the men's interactions without actually taking part himself, but this produced some ethical problems, as participants weren't aware that he was researching them.

(e) This is a relevant study well applied.

James Patrick also went undercover, in a Glasgow gang. He could not have done this research using methods like questionnaires or structured interviews, as the boys in the gang would not have answered questions on their behaviour. But again, he deceived the gang and he became involved in deviant behaviour. Ethical considerations often force researchers to use overt observation.

(e) This is another relevant and well-applied study and the ethical dimension is introduced.

Some feminist researchers argue that it is important to make relationships with the people being researched. This is the case with Anne Oakley in *From Here to Maternity*, when she told the pregnant women that she was a researcher. In her study, she helped the women to get information from the hospital, so she was able to give something back to them in return for her researching them. So in conclusion, there are many practical, ethical and theoretical factors that affect the choice of method. It is difficult to say which is the most important, but funding is certainly very significant.

🄔 This is another well-applied and relevant study. There is also a short conclusion that tries to evaluate the importance of factors affecting choice.

🄔 18/20 marks awarded. **Overall, this is a competent, coherent and well-structured essay. Practical and theoretical factors are dealt with very well, but at the expense of ethical issues.**

# Paper 3 **Education**

**Read Item A below and answer questions 01 to 04 that follow.**

## Item A

It is argued that some teachers can make a difference to whether a student is successful in education or not. There is a great deal of sociological evidence to show that if teachers demonstrate negative attitudes towards some students this can affect the self-esteem and educational progress of those students. This labelling process, where it is successful, can result in a self-fulfilling prophecy. Some of these labels are based on the teachers' values and attitudes to social class. Some students who are seen as having more cultural capital than others are likely to be treated more positively by their teachers.

**(01) Explain what is meant by the term 'cultural capital'.**                  (2 marks)

ⓔ You should be familiar with this concept, but don't confuse it with *material* capital.

**(02) Suggest three ways in which schooling may be seen to be ethnocentric.**          (6 marks)

ⓔ This shows the importance of your knowledge and understanding. If you don't know the term you will lose 6 marks.

**(03) Outline some of the ways in which schooling mirrors the world of work.**          (12 marks)

ⓔ You need to use the correspondence principle here and give two to three well-developed aspects of it.

**(04) Using material from Item A and elsewhere, assess the view that labelling is the major cause of pupils' underachievement.**                                (20 marks)

ⓔ This requires you to demonstrate your evaluation skills. You must weigh up evidence showing that labelling is the major cause and contrast it with factors that other theorists would consider to be more significant.

### C- grade student

**(01)** This is where middle-class pupils do better at school because they have more money to buy things for school.

ⓔ **0/2 marks awarded.** The student confuses cultural with material capital. He/she should have developed the 'things for school' point to score.

**(02)** This is where white is seen as better. It happens in the way subjects like history are taught.

ⓔ **1/6 marks awarded.** The student is aware of the concept, but is unable to point to specific ways. The reference to history can be linked to 'white', making it a partial explanation. Always read the question carefully and make sure that you do what the question asks.

**(03)** Willis said that school teaches working-class kids how to get working-class jobs. He studied two groups of working-class boys, one called 'the lads' and the other called 'the ear'oles'. The lads spent their time at school having a 'laff' and messed around. The lads thought that school was really boring and messed around to make the teachers angry. They left school without any qualifications and so went into dead-end jobs. When they were in work Willis said that they were still messing around but the system needed workers in dead-end jobs.

ⓔ **5/12 marks awarded.** The student has shown some reasonable knowledge and understanding appropriate to the question but the answer is not as well focused as it might be. It only offers one implicit way (the boredom of schooling and the boredom of dead-end jobs) in which schooling mirrors the world of work. There is very limited analysis/evaluation.

**(04)** Labelling means that teachers treat some students differently from others. They may label them as 'lazy', 'troublemaker' and 'clown' etc. This could cause a self-fulfilling prophecy. This means that the students come to believe the label and it sticks so they fail. Labelling theory is part of an interactionist view and Becker studied it.

ⓔ The student demonstrates some reasonable knowledge and understanding of the process of labelling and the self-fulfilling prophecy.

Hargreaves' study showed that teachers make judgements about pupils from the beginning. They call some pupils lazy, good, bad, troublesome etc. These labels affect a pupil because if he or she is labelled as a troublemaker this will affect their feelings about themselves and about how they see school. He also said that setting and streaming were bad for students, because if you are in the bottom set then you will feel like a failure and the teachers will treat you differently. Then you are likely to give up and fail.

The television programme *The Eye of the Storm* showed that when the teacher put collars on the pupils and treated them differently because of the colour of their eyes, their test results went down. Interactionists believe that people live up to their labels, which makes a self-fulfilling prophecy, and some labels are harder to get rid of than others. This is called a master status.

ⓔ This paragraph starts well with appropriate sociological evidence. The reference to the television programme is rather simplistic and does not draw out the implications of the experiment in sufficient detail. The student makes useful reference to other in-school processes.

> Becker believes that teachers have a view of the 'ideal pupil'. These pupils are middle class and hardworking. Teachers have different expectations of these pupils and encourage them to succeed and so they do. He showed that teachers have stereotypes of pupils and they don't treat all pupils the same. Ray Rist's study of the tigers, cardinals and clowns supports Becker's views. The study showed that 'What teachers believe, their students achieve'. Rist said that the teacher's labelling of the kindergarten children was based on their appearance and behaviour. Rist went back at the end of a year and the children were still in the same groups. This shows that labelling is very strong. So labelling is very important in the success of pupils, but home factors are important too.
>
> In conclusion, some sociologists believe that many students fail, especially black boys, due to teachers' labelling, but a study of black girls showed that they were successful because they resisted the teacher's racist label of them as failures. Marxists like Willis would say that other factors are more important, like working-class children are prepared for working-class jobs.

ⓔ **14/20 marks awarded.** This is a sound response. The student demonstrates some relevant knowledge and understanding of the labelling process and applies some studies. It is mainly descriptive and there is some evaluation and analysis. The student is aware that there are criticisms of the labelling process, but these need to be developed further.

### A-grade student

**(01)** Middle-class pupils do better at school because they have the right attitudes and values from their parents. Parents know more about the education system and can work it to their advantage, like paying for private tuition for their children.

ⓔ **2/2 marks awarded.** Although the example given isn't strictly cultural capital, as it refers to economic capital, the student's response is sufficient to score full marks.

**(02)** Where schooling is ethnocentric it is biased towards white culture. History may only refer to black experience in terms of slavery. Literature would be European/white and religion would be based on Christianity. There may be tokenism as well, where festivals are celebrated once a year. This has sometimes been referred to as 'saris, samosas and steel bands'.

ⓔ **6/6 marks awarded.** This response is full and has more than three ways that schooling may be seen as ethnocentric. The student clearly understands the concepts.

**(03)** Sociologists argue that there are many ways that schooling mirrors the world of work. Functionalists say that schooling prepares individuals for work to make them into efficient workers. This is for the benefit of society. However, Marxists say that schooling is really for the benefit of the capitalist system and pupils are taught to become obedient workers at school.

Bowles and Gintis argued that the economy cast a long shadow over school. They say school operates to the correspondence principle. This means that schools really work to meet the needs of capitalists. B & G say pupils learn lots of different subjects at school and the day is broken up into these subjects so that students have no control over their day or how they learn. B & G compare this to the experience of work, in which workers are disempowered.

Through the hidden curriculum pupils learn the values of capitalist society. For example, they learn to be obedient to authority, to be disciplined, to put up with boredom and to compete with others. B & G say that this prepares them to be docile workers. However, from an interpretivist's perspective, this does not take into account the reality of school life. Pupils do not necessarily accept what teachers say and many actively resist and rebel.

**ⓔ 12/12 marks awarded.** This response is well focused on the question. There is good knowledge and understanding of sociological arguments and the student demonstrates explicit analysis and evaluation.

**(04)** Some sociologists such as interactionists argue that processes inside schools, especially labelling, play the most important role in a pupil's success or failure in education. Because interactionists focus on interactions between individuals, they are especially interested in the relationship between teachers and pupils and how this affects the achievement of the pupils. However, other sociologists would argue that labelling is only one factor and they see the structure of the education system and social class background as more important. As Item A states 'Some students who are seen as having more cultural capital than others are likely to be treated more positively by their teachers.'

**ⓔ** This is a sound start. It is well focused and provides the theoretical context to labelling and introduces a criticism from a conflict perspective. The student also uses material from the item in an evaluative way, to support the criticism of labelling.

Hargreaves, a labelling theorist, looked at how the processes within schools affected the success or failure of pupils. He examined the effects of streaming on boys' success. Placed in the lowest stream of a secondary modern school the boys felt like failures. In order to cope with this feeling they acted up in class and challenged the authority of their teachers. Hargreaves also showed us that teachers type pupils in a three-stage process of speculation, elaboration and finally stabilisation.

**ⓔ** This paragraph examines streaming, another in-school process which is linked to labelling, but the way this happens isn't made clear here. The final sentence could have been linked to streaming more directly.

One important study linked to labelling is Rosenthal and Jacobson's. They lied to teachers that they had a test that could identify 'spurters' (children who would do well). They came back a year later and tested again. They found that the 'spurters' had generally scored more highly than the rest. R & J argued that this was due to teacher expectations. However, as they did not spend any time observing the classes to see how the teachers behaved to their pupils, they couldn't prove what had gone on. Both the validity of their IQ test and their findings have been criticised.

(e) This student demonstrates appropriate knowledge and understanding, which is well applied and evaluated.

Rist's research of a kindergarten class is also focused on labelling. By the end of their first week at nursery, the teacher had placed the 5-year-olds on three separate tables named the tigers, cardinals and clowns. Rist argued that pupils were labelled on the basis of appearance and how they spoke rather than their abilities. The seating did not change for the rest of the year and the tigers did much better than the others. Rist concluded that 'what teachers believe, their pupils achieve'.

Some students may get labelled more negatively than others. Gillborn said that Afro-Caribbean students were more likely to receive negative labels from staff. Teachers tended to stereotype the boys as unruly and disrespectful. The boys were seen as more challenging and difficult to control and they were dealt with more harshly than other boys were. The Afro-Caribbean boys saw this as unfair and as a result lived up to the negative stereotype.

(e) The student has demonstrated sound knowledge and understanding of several empirical studies in this area. However, the question asks whether labelling is the major cause of pupils' underachievement and this is not addressed directly.

In conclusion, critics of the interactionist approach see it as too deterministic, but not all interactionists accept this deterministic view of labelling. Margaret Fuller's research on black girls showed that they were able to resist the labels of their teachers and achieve despite them. Mac an Ghaill also showed the process to be more complex, where students often ignored those staff they felt were being racist towards them. We can see that although labelling plays a very important role in students' achievement, it is important to say that other factors, such as material and cultural deprivation will also play a part in this process. So we cannot say that labelling is the main factor.

(e) 17/20 marks awarded. **These paragraphs together with the conclusion, provide excellent sociological evidence on labelling, but it is not always well focused on the question on labelling and underachievement. The conclusion introduces us to the other factors that have a part to play in educational success and makes use of the item.**

# Methods in context

This question requires you to apply your knowledge and understanding of sociological research methods to the study of this particular issue in education.

Read Item B and answer the question that follows.

## Item B

### Researching anti-school subcultures

Not all children respond to schooling in the same way. Individual children attach different meanings to school and relate in different ways to the school experience. Often, teachers treat some groups of children differently from others, and attach negative labels to them. In some cases the response to this differential treatment from teachers results in resistance and even the development of anti-school subcultures.

Some sociologists prefer methods that produce qualitative data, such as participant observation. This method allows them to see how members of groups really behave together rather than using interviews where they might not be truthful. As researchers are generally unable to disguise themselves as pupils, covert participant observation is unlikely; it would also be unethical.

Another approach would be to use questionnaires. These could be self-completed in the classroom or sent to pupils' homes. They reach a wide audience and produce data that can show patterns and trends. However, people do not always give truthful responses.

(05) **Using material from Item B and elsewhere, assess the strengths and limitations of one of the following methods for the study of anti-school subcultures:**
   (i) **questionnaires**
   (ii) **participant observation**                                              (20 marks)

   ⓔ Don't fall into the trap of describing any studies here. Even if a particular study may be relevant, the specific method might not be. Concentrate on your chosen method and apply it to this issue. Always think of the research characteristics of subjects, researchers and the educational environment.

**C- grade student**

(05) (ii) In order to study pupil subcultures at first hand, many sociologists would choose participant observation (PO) as their method. There are two types of PO, covert and overt. Covert means that the observer is hidden, but in overt the observer tells the subjects what they are doing in the research. Paul Willis used PO to study working-class lads in school. He was overt because he was too old to pretend to be a student. He studied 12 boys called the 'lads'. Willis was able to see the lads' behaviour for himself. They liked to mess around and 'have a laff'.

ⓔ The student has identified two types of PO and given an example of an appropriate study. There is also an advantage of PO given (Level I).

According to Item B not all pupils are treated in the same way by their teachers and this may result in subcultures. Hargreaves showed that setting and streaming caused pupil subcultures. Children in lower streams have lower self-esteem and start to hate school because they feel themselves to be failures. This makes them turn against school and reject its values.

ⓔ The student is producing Level 0 information on the issue itself. This will not score highly. The question asks for strengths and limitations of PO and as yet the student has failed to provide this.

Interactionists see PO as a valid method because you can get very close to the truth. Willis could not have gained the same information if he had given the lads a questionnaire to fill in as they would not have taken it seriously. However, it might be dangerous to use PO with these groups. You don't know if they are violent and even if the researcher is overt, there is the possibility of them rejecting him as they might think he's on the side of the school against them.

**Examiner tip**

This could have become Level 3 if the student had made reference, perhaps, to heads not wanting the reputation of the school damaged by acknowledging the existence of anti-school subcultures within their school.

ⓔ This paragraph is more focused. Reference is made to theory and there is some contrast evaluation on the problems of questionnaires. There is a Level 3 point about the nature of the group and potential danger to the researcher.

If the researcher wants to research in classrooms, they have to be able to gain access to the school. Headteachers don't often let researchers in as with league tables, they need to make sure there's no time being wasted in lessons.
Teachers would also have to give permission to have someone observe their lessons. With overt PO, there is the problem of Hawthorne effect as the pupils might deliberately mess around in class if they know the researcher is watching them.

**Examiner tip**

The student comes to an abrupt end. It is always worthwhile writing a conclusion in order to gain more marks for evaluation.

ⓔ **14/20 marks awarded. Although some of this response is tangential to the question, the student does focus at times. The answer scores Level 0 for the subject**

matter of the issue without relevance to method; Level 1 for theory and some strengths and limitations. There are two Level 2 points for gatekeepers (heads and teachers) and a Level 3 point (undeveloped) on danger to the researcher.

**A-grade student**

**(05) (i)** At first sight questionnaires are not the most obvious choice of research method for the topic of anti-school subcultures. However, sometimes the funding body insists that a quantitative method should be used despite the researcher's preferences.

**e** This is a very good opening paragraph to the essay. This would be a highly unusual response, but already the student has caught the attention of the examiner.

Questionnaires are simply pre-set schedules of questions which are given to all respondents in exactly the same way. This makes the method highly reliable and is favoured by positivists because they are considered to be both objective and valid. As Item B says, questionnaires allow researchers to gain a much larger response from a wider sample.

**e** This paragraph contains Level 1 points on method, including theoretical location.

School research involves getting permission from schools to research the pupils. This may be a problem. Willis was refused access many times and finally had to take on a role in the school youth club before the head allowed him in. Also the topic of anti-school subcultures would be a problem. Heads don't want their schools to get a bad reputation, especially if the research is published in the local paper. They might lose parental support. If the questionnaires were given to pupils to complete in the classroom, those who were anti-school would be less likely to tell the truth as it might get them into trouble with the head teacher. There's also the problem of who will read their responses? If the school insists on looking at the forms, pupils are unlikely to write truthful answers. Another problem with self-completed questionnaires is that the language may be too complex for the pupils to understand. Research shows that it is usually disengaged working-class pupils (like the 'lads') who join these anti-school groups. It is possible that they may not understand what is being asked and just to show off, they might write nonsense or rude responses.

**e** The student demonstrates excellent knowledge and understanding of the chosen method and its advantages. It is located theoretically and evaluated. There are several Level 3 points made here:
- heads not wanting a bad reputation for their school for having any anti-school subcultures exposed
- bad publicity = loss of parental support — linked to the above point on anti-school subcultures
- anti-school pupils lying about their involvement — getting into trouble
- language difficulties (disengaged students might have literacy problems)

Not many sociologists would use a questionnaire to gain information on subcultures. By their very nature, subcultures are not accessible. Interactionists would dismiss questionnaire data as invalid. They would say that we cannot get close to social reality by simply imposing the researcher's constructs on the people being studied. Questionnaire design reflects the values of the researcher. Even for positivists, questionnaires would be more useful for collecting factual data, such as social class, qualifications, attitudes to school and parental background, than for understanding subcultures.

(e) The student demonstrates a sophisticated evaluation and analysis of method. It is impressive to see that he/she refers to an in-house criticism of positivists.

In conclusion, it is clear that questionnaires are not the most appropriate method to gain an understanding of the reality of school subcultures. They may produce a lot of data but they do not capture the social reality of those involved because, as Weber said, sociologists need to use verstehen.

(e) **20/20 marks awarded. This is an extremely sophisticated, conceptually detailed and well-structured response that will gain full marks. There is evidence of P, E and T here and some well-developed Level 3 points.**

# Research methods

> These questions permit you to draw examples from any areas of sociology with which you are familiar.

**(06)** Explain what is meant by the term 'sampling unit'. (2 marks)

> ℮ Don't confuse this with 'sampling frame'. It is important to learn the terms relating to sampling.

**(07)** Suggest two types of sampling technique. (4 marks)

> ℮ This time you need to give two types of technique. Here although the word 'random' would be correct, it would be safer to write 'random sampling'.

**(08)** Suggest two reasons why some sociologists choose to collect qualitative data. (4 marks)

> ℮ This is a methodological question. 'Validity' on its own would not score, but 'higher validity' would gain 2 marks.

**(09)** Examine the problems sociologists may face in using different kinds of secondary data in their research. (20 marks)

> ℮ It is essential to focus on problems rather than strengths and limitations of the data. Remember to examine both qualitative and quantitative data here.

### C- grade student

**(06)** As on the electoral register = one person on the list.

> ℮ **1/2 marks awarded.** The student has given an example rather than a definition, but it is a correct one.

**(07)** Snowball sampling
Random sampling

> ℮ **4/4 marks awarded.** Two correct techniques given.

**(08)** More valued
They want *verstehen*
More truthful data

> ℮ **4/4 marks awarded.** 'More valued' does not score but there are two other appropriate reasons here so full marks can be given.

**(09)** Secondary data can be used by all kinds of sociologists. Positivists use secondary quantitative data such as official statistics and interpretivists use them to get qualitative data, from historical and personal documents such as diaries and letters.

ⓔ The paragraph introduces the concept and gives appropriate examples. There is reference to theoretical location but it is not developed.

Laslett did a survey on the family — he wanted to know how the size of the family changed over time and he used secondary sources like parish records. This was good because it was a survey of the past and all the people were dead. However, there are problems because Laslett couldn't really test how true the records were. They were usually collected by clergymen who might not have taken accurate data. Also, some of the births may not have been recorded, as they were illegitimate.

ⓔ This is a relevant study and has some appropriate evaluation but it lacks major concepts. There is good focus on problems of the data.

Although Anne Frank's diary is valid because she wrote down her personal experiences at the time, it isn't representative, because she was a middle-class girl and she wouldn't have known what it was like for working-class families. It's not reliable either because we only have one diary. We cannot compare her family's experiences with any others, but without her account we would have little understanding of what they went through.

ⓔ Again, this is a useful example with evaluation and relevant concepts. There is a tendency here to slip into an advantages vs disadvantages response.

Positivists like official statistics because they say that they are valid and reliable, but interpretivists wouldn't agree. Positivists say that as the government produces them, we can trust them and sociologists wouldn't be able to do without these figures. Interpretivists argue that they are sometimes made up by governments to look good, like crime and unemployment statistics, and even league tables have problems. So we can see there are problems with these data. However, there are some advantages as well as they are free or cheap and available and some are in statistical tables.

ⓔ There is contrast here between the major perspectives, but the inclusion of examples to illustrate the problems of official statistics would be rewarded.

ⓔ 13/20 marks awarded. **Overall, there is reasonable knowledge and understanding, but the focus is not always clear. The student has produced a 'strengths versus limitations' response rather than one focused only on problems. However, there are several points raised and the student refers to theory, some concepts, one appropriate study and one example.**

**A- grade student**

**(06)** A sampling unit is one person/household/business etc. from a sampling frame. It could be one pupil on the school register.

ⓔ **2/2 marks awarded.** This is a sound definition and includes an appropriate example as well.

**(07)** Quota sampling
Stratified random sampling
Non-representative (the affluent worker)

ⓔ **4/4 marks awarded.** Any two from the three listed would score full marks.

**(08)** Interpretivists prefer this type of data as it is highly valid because it is more meaningful, more in-depth and gives insight.

ⓔ **4/4 marks awarded.** 'Interpretivists prefer it' would not score, as it is not a reason. However, the student has also given three other appropriate reasons and any two would count.

**(09)** Secondary data are collected by another researcher for another purpose. Using secondary data, such as historical documents and diaries and letters of the time, may be the only way to examine the past, but we have to be very careful in terms of validity and reliability. Although there are many advantages to using secondary data (like cost-effectiveness, as they are often free or cheap, easy to get hold of, cover the past and in many different types), we are going to look at the problems with them.

ⓔ This is a good introduction that demonstrates knowledge and understanding and is already focused on problems. However, to conflate validity and reliability like this will not score marks.

Personal documents will not be reliable as they are mainly one-offs, like a letter or a diary of one individual. They could lack authenticity and be fakes, like Hitler's diaries, or they could be someone's fantasy of what their lives were really like. A politician's diary is likely to show the best side of the person, rather than revealing that they had been involved in anything that might damage their reputation.

ⓔ There is a selection of possible problems here, with some analysis.

Even though these data may save time from not having to collect primary data, you may have to go through loads of documents to find anything that's relevant to the present research. There aren't so many ethical problems compared with some primary data, but sometimes you may be using personal documents without the individual's permission, and you may be being insensitive to the feelings of other family members by publishing the data.

(e)  There are both practical and ethical criticisms here; the latter are often ignored in a question like this.

> Theoretically, all researchers can use secondary data, but there are problems. Positivists use official statistics because they say that they are social facts, but interpretivists argue that there's the 'dark figure' with soft statistics such as crime and unemployment. Durkheim used suicide statistics in his study, but he assumed that the figures were correct and later researchers have criticised him for not treating them as being socially constructed. But without statistics it would have been impossible for Durkheim to go around collecting all the data for himself. Official statistics are also open to the accusation of manipulation, as past governments have massaged the figures to make themselves look good, or changed definitions such as eligibility for unemployment to reduce the overall figures.

(e)  This is a very good paragraph. The reference to 'soft' statistics is sound and the student has developed the argument well.

> We know that criminal statistics are those reported and recorded, but the dark figure is unknown. With rape, for example, less than 5% of people accused of rape get convicted. Feminists argue that many victims are afraid to tell the police and so the majority of rapists go free.
>
> Marxists see other problems as they say that official statistics are not to be trusted because they reinforce the ideology of the ruling class, by focusing on the crimes of the working class rather than corporate and white-collar crimes.

(e)  These are two important criticisms and each is well developed.

> Although there are many problems with secondary data, John Scott said they are useful as long as we take into account their authenticity (are they what they say they are?), their credibility (can we believe them?), their representativeness (can we use them to generalise?), and their meaning (can we be sure we know what they mean?).

(e)  18/20 marks awarded. **Overall, the essay is well focused on the question. It has an evaluative tone and there are practical and ethical problems and sound theoretical argument.**

# Paper 4 Education

These questions are for you to attempt yourself. There are examiner comments for each question.

Read Item A below and answer questions 01 to 04 that follow.

## Item A

A number of recent government policies have been introduced in order to make the education system more market-orientated. These policies include more parental choice, the introduction of league tables and academies and changes in funding arrangements. Some sociologists have argued that the effect of these policies has been to produce a more unequal educational system.

Changes in the relationship between schools and parents have been especially beneficial for middle-class parents. It is argued that as the power of the local education authorities has declined, so middle-class parents have exploited the situation in the interests of their own children. Working-class parents tend not to have the knowledge and skills needed to influence decisions over which schools their children attend. Consequently, middle-class students fill the more desirable and usually more successful schools.

---

**(01) Explain what is meant by the term 'ethnocentric' curriculum.** (2 marks)

ⓔ It is a good idea to give the definition and add an example, e.g. 'Literature will only be the study of white British or European authors'. If your definition is incorrect, you would score 1 mark for a correct example.

**(02) Suggest three material factors that may be responsible for working-class underachievement at school.** (6 marks)

ⓔ Watch here that you are giving **material factors** and don't confuse them with **cultural factors** such as parental values. Material factors relate to economic issues.

**(03) Outline some of the reasons why males are underachieving in the education system.** (12 marks)

ⓔ Here you must concentrate on reasons for males' underachievement rather than females' achievement. For instance, laddism and 'boys are too cool for school'. Remember, 'the education system' includes colleges and universities as well as schools.

**(04) Using material from Item A and elsewhere, assess the view that the marketisation of education has created greater inequality in education.** (20 marks)

ⓔ If you are not familiar with marketisation, refer back to the sections on policies in education. The 1988 Education Act and more recent Labour and coalition government policies are helpful. Think of some evidence that would suggest that some of the policies have benefited working-class pupils as well as middle-class ones. The assessment skills here are AO1 = 8 marks and AO2 = 12 marks.

# Methods in context

> **This question requires you to apply your knowledge and understanding of sociological research methods to the study of this particular issue in education.**
>
> **Read Item B and answer the question that follows.**

## Item B

Many social commentators argue that social class is still the most important factor in the differences in students' achievement. Even though various governments have attempted to create equality through their policies, social class continues to advantage some students and to disadvantage others. Some sociologists maintain that the educational attainment gap between the classes was as great in 2007 as it was 50 or 100 years ago.

Use of the case study method allows researchers to make use of several methods for their research. These can be both qualitative and quantitative. The case study method does not allow for generalisation.

Structured or formal interviews can reach a wide population and in educational research, they can be conducted at home with pupils and their parents. They may also be conducted with teachers to examine their views. However, there is always the problem of the interviewer effect.

---

**(05) Using material from Item B and elsewhere, assess the strengths and limitations of one of the following methods for the study of social-class background on pupil achievement:**
  **(i)  case study**
  **(ii) structured interviews**                                                (20 marks)

---

Read Item B carefully and think about the relationship between social class background and educational achievement. You must apply your method to the *issue* — what specific strengths and limitations would be relevant? These score at Level 3.

Always use the material in the item. With any question that asks you to assess usefulness, think practical, ethical and theoretical (PET) factors.

Some areas to think about:

Case study: multiple methods can be used to compare one school (or neighbourhood) with another — to research different social class groups. Expensive on time and money, greater insight, depth, different types of methods available — strengths and limitations of each.

Structured interviews: quick, relatively cheap, reliability, response rate (conducted at home), validity, interviewer effect, sensitivity of issue, social desirability, social class differences, cultural capital, and material deprivation, misunderstandings, language codes.

Research settings and subjects:

- Access to schools, heads, teachers, homes and parents, other possible contacts — permission, openness/deception, CRB tested.
- Pupils and parents — how will methods suit them? — think how social class differences might affect the data: sensitivity, language codes. Where will the interviews be conducted?
- Researcher's characteristics for case study: c/overt PO = possibly teacher-in-disguise, interviewer, non-participant observer etc.

AO1 skills = 8 marks and AO2 skills = 12 marks

# Research methods

> These questions permit you to draw examples from any areas of sociology
> with which you are familiar.

**(06) Explain what is meant by the term 'hypothesis'.**      (2 marks)

ℯ Do not forget to bring in the idea of 'testing' a statement.

**(07) Suggest one advantage and one disadvantage of the longitudinal survey as a
research method.**      (4 marks)

ℯ Make sure that you are clear what a longitudinal survey is. Many students confuse it with
participant observation.

**(08) Suggest two reasons why interpretivists reject the use of official statistics in research.**      (4 marks)

ℯ Be clear that you refer to interpretivists specifically. Make sure that you focus on official
statistics, not simply quantitative data.

**(09) Examine the reasons why sociologists rarely use the laboratory method in research.**      (20 marks)

ℯ It is essential that you look at 'reasons' why it is *rarely used*, rather than the strengths and
limitations of the method.

Structure your answer in terms of practical, ethical and theoretical (PET) factors. Look at the
reasons why positivistic sociologists might justify the laboratory method, even though they might
not choose to use it themselves.

Studies that you might refer to are those of Milgram, Bandura et al. and Zimbardo. Use them to
show why sociologists reject the method (the interpretivist critique).

Practical reasons: artificiality; sampling; control over variables; Hawthorne effect; demand
characteristics and social desirability.

Ethical reasons: BSA guidelines oppose any research that might place subjects at risk of short-term
or long-term effects. Field and natural experiments are used instead by sociologists and this would
show evaluation skills.

AO1 skills = 10 marks, AO2 = 10 marks

## Knowledge check answers

1 A system of shared values that underpin society.

2 A system whereby individuals are judged not on their background but by their talent and effort.

3 Possible answers include: obedience to authority; fragmentation of the school day; punctuality; acceptance of hierarchy; extrinsic rewards, e.g. qualifications; pupils' lack of power about the subjects taught and the organisation of the school day.

4 A set of ideas and beliefs that justify the position of the powerful in society and are accepted by the less powerful.

5 A system whereby power is held in male hands. All the major social institutions operate in the interests of men. Feminists argue that women suffer multiple disadvantages in a patriarchal system.

6 Possible answers include: Ofsted inspections; publication of league tables; greater diversity of schools (or specialist schools or academies or free schools); parental choice; National Curriculum producing standardisation; competition between schools for high achieving pupils.

7 Possible answers include: the introduction of free schools; increases in university tuition fees up to £9,000; the E-Bac at GCSE; allowing ex-service personnel to teach without gaining a full teaching qualification.

8 (a) Streaming is where the organisation of pupils within school is based on their 'measured' abilities. There are usually three streams, high, middle and lower, and pupils are taught all subjects in their specific stream. Setting occurs when pupils, on the basis of their measured ability, are placed in different classes in specific subjects, e.g. mathematics and languages.
(b) The self-fulfilling prophecy exists when a label is successfully attached by a person in authority (e.g. teacher) to someone (e.g. pupil), and the person labelled comes to accept their label and behave accordingly.

9 This is seen as a cause of educational underachievement of pupils from working-class and some ethnic minority backgrounds. It is linked to conditions of poverty, such as: poor housing, lack of space to study, poor diets, and lack of money to buy educational resources.

10 Possible answers include: different clothes and toys for girls and boys; ascribing different characteristics to girls and boys and behaving towards them on this basis (e.g. boys don't cry, girls are more emotionally caring); channelling students into assumed gender-appropriate subjects, for instance girls into more 'feminine' subjects, assuming they won't like to study science and mathematics. Although the National Curriculum made core subjects compulsory, there is still evidence that boys and girls opt for different subjects by choice.

11 Possible answers include: studying subjects like sciences and maths that were previously seen as traditionally male, and achieving highly in those subjects; achieving high marks for the coursework element of many subjects; achieving higher percentage passes than boys overall and staying on to study at AS/A-level.

12 An institution is described as institutionally racist if its policies and personnel discriminate against a particular minority group.

13 This means that each part of the system (or school in this case) is viewed as having equal value.

14 (a) Theoretical means relating to a body of knowledge that seeks to understand society. Empirical means that an idea is tested in the real world.
(b) Social actor means the individual who takes part in social action.

15 Objectivity means to be impartial and without bias and subjectivity means the individual's (or researcher's) own opinions and values, which can influence the research process and outcomes.

16 Primary data are collected by the researchers themselves. Secondary data are used by sociologists in their research but they did not collect them themselves.

17 Possible answers include: lack of informed consent; deception of subjects; access to information that might implicate subjects in crime.

18 'Authenticity' of secondary data means whether or not it is true of the person who created it. Some documents may be fakes and sociologists need to be sure that the data they have are genuine.